The Grand Prix Book of Motor Racing Quotations

Also by Eugene Weber

The Book of Business Quotations
The Book of Snooker and Billiards Quotations
(with Clive Everton)

THE GRAND PRIX BOOK OF MOTOR RACING QUOTATIONS

Eugene Weber

Hodder & Stoughton

First published in Great Britain in 1995 by Hodder and Stoughton
A division of Hodder Headline PLC

British Library Cataloguing in Publication Data

Weber, Eugene
Grand Prix Book of Motor Racing Quotations
I. Title II. Tristram, Geoff
796.72

ISBN 0 340 63748 X

Typeset by Hewer Text Composition Services, Edinburgh
Printed and bound in Great Britain by
Mackays of Chatham PLC, Chatham, Kent

Hodder and Stoughton
A division of Hodder Headline PLC
338 Euston Road
London NW1 3BH

CONTENTS

Introduction	vii
Acknowledgements	viii
Cars	1
Circuits	6
Commentators	8
Constructors	13
Design	15
Drivers	20
Emotions	33
Failure	34
Fear	35
Ferrari	36
Formula One	39
Friends	42
Fuel	44
IndyCar	46
Mechanics	50
The Media	53
Money	55
Needle	59
Nicknames	66
Nostalgia	69
The Powers That Be	72
Pressure	73
Problems	75
Racing	78
Retirement	102
Safety	108

Sayings   112
Self-Image   114
Shunts   119
Spares   134
Spectators   165
Sponsorship   166
Technology   169
Winning   170
Wives and Girlfriends   181
Youth   186
Last Word   191

Index   193

INTRODUCTION

Some books of quotations are intended to amuse, and some are meant to enlighten. This book, I hope, will do both.

Few years in the history of motor racing have seen such excitement but such tragedy as 1994, with the loss of Ayrton Senna and Roland Ratzenberger. Yet the strange mixture of stark death and side-splitting humour have been a feature of racing parlance for decades.

Although I have naturally concentrated on Grand Prix racing, my voluminous research has taken me across the whole spectrum of the sport, including such branches as rallying, stock-car racing and even truck racing, and I have included quotations from as wide a variety of people as possible – drivers, owners, spectators, wives, girlfriends, media, the church, a couple of rock stars and a boxer, as well as John Major's former caterer.

I hope I have succeeded in capturing the spirit of a glorious sport.

Eugene Weber, 1995

ACKNOWLEDGEMENTS

I would like to express my gratitude to the following people who have helped me to compile this collection: Colin Webb, Editor-in-Chief of PA News, for permission to use the PA's Newspaper Library. The book could not be completed without it. Thanks are also due to Katarina Shelley, Deputy Librarian at PA News, and her husband Martin. Simon Skelly, Project Engineer at PA News, and John Churchman, Editorial Systems Manager, also at PA News, were especially helpful.

I would also like to record my thanks to Vivienne Schweikert, Paul and Tony Hannon, John Vincent of the *Irish Times*, and Michael Daly of the *Irish Independent*, Jeff Care, Juliette Langford of the Royal Automobile Club for allowing me access to their excellent library and Geoff Tristram for his witty and apt cartoons.

Finally, I am deeply indebted to Nigel Roebuck of Autosport for reading the manuscript.

CARS

God created man in His own image, and that was considered the noblest of all creations; now man is creating something, the regularity and concord of whose working are beginning to rival his own. Each part of a racing car has its own function, which it has to perform without fail and coordinate with all the other parts without fail, so that the efficiency in one department need not be sacrificed to efficiency in another, and speed may be consistent with endurance. It is the same with a man; and, as in a man, so in a car, perfect combination of all the members is the aim.

Sir Tim Birkin, *Full Throttle*

I still feel for our Alfa the adolescent tenderness of first love, the immaculate affection for the mamma.

Enzo Ferrari, on the Alfa Romeo that was conceived during his time with the team

Grand Prix cars are very close-fitting – you put them on, more or less, as you would a glove. You wear the car. The car is an extension of yourself.

Graham Hill

The talent required to drive a machine to the ultimate of its ability is the same, the same inherent chemical element is present today as when the sport began. Machines exist to be interpreted and understood.

Jackie Stewart

Small cars for small-minded people.

   Innes Ireland, on modern-day racing

A driver's relationship with his car is something very sensitive. You must be feeling exactly what the car is feeling and constantly adapt yourself to the way the car is. It is like the car is an extension of your body.

   Emerson Fittipaldi

Fear is not a stupid thing. Winning is not a question of courage, but of faith in oneself and in the car. A car is like a creature that lives, with its own emotions and its own heart. You have to understand it and love it accordingly. I knew many drivers more courageous than me. They are dead now.

   Juan Fangio

The Formula One car cannot speak. It has hundreds of moving parts, delicately interdependent, all of which can and do sometimes go wrong. It is an inbred, snorting, snarling strain of motoring genealogy, whose fuel consumption is prodigious, whose noise is deafening, and whose bodywork has more to do with origami than common roadworthiness. Standing idle in the pits it reminds the cynical observer of a grounded pterodactyl, unadapted for anything outside its own loony world. But, set in motion, it becomes the fast and terrifying god that all men recognise, and little boys dream of imposing their will upon.

   Angela Patmore, *Sportsmen Under Stress*

I think of this car as a duck. Quiet, stately and calm above the water line, frantically paddling below.

   Ron Dennis, on the MP4/7

CARS

The noise of the engine is a sickening, ear-splitting whine. It is a horrifying noise, a noise you cannot imagine outside war.

William Leith, journalist

I need again that almost trembling feeling when I stand beside the car that you have when you see the woman in your life that you are crazy for.

Ayrton Senna

My racing team spends millions of dollars to make these fabulous toys for me to play with – and then pays me lots of money to drive.

Nelson Piquet

If Darwin were alive today he might choose as the perfect example of selective breeding neither pigeons nor dogs, but an inanimate object: the grand prix racing car. From that first internal combustion engine which is the common ancestor of all cars, it has been developed with one end in view, to maximise its performance.

Andro Linklater, journalist

It is not a question of what you are going to do with the car but what the car is going to do with you.

Tony Vandervell

You must become just part of its machinery. But I have to admit I am the most vital piece of the car.

Niki Lauda

3

The next one.

Enzo Ferrari, replying when asked which was his favourite car

Cars are like girls. I get the same thrill from a beautiful car as I do from a beautiful girl, the thrill of getting them to respond. An ordinary family saloon is as different from a racing car as a girl guide is from a dolly.

Stirling Moss

A new motor comes into the world with the cry of a newborn child.

Enzo Ferrari

If you treat a car like a woman, if you relate it to a woman because it is a very highly strung and nervous piece of equipment, you can have this love affair with it. You have got to be able to understand it and comprehend its feelings and habits. You have to coax it sometimes to get the best out of it; you have to caress it and treat it gently. At other times, maybe on a different circuit, you have to give it a really good thrashing because that is the only way it understands, because its personality does not suit that particular occasion or track.

Jackie Stewart

I believe that every man has a special place in his heart for one woman above all others and also for one car. In my case I think that probably my E-type Jaguar was the most satisfying and exciting car in my life.

Prince Michael of Kent

In a race they are always dying, even if they win. It is unbearable.

Enzo Ferrari (Brock Yates, *Enzo Ferrari*)

I build my cars to go, not stop.

Ettore Bugatti, responding to criticism of his brakes (Ivan Rendall, *The Power and the Glory*)

To me, racing cars are marvellous things sent from God.

Gil de Ferran

During a race, it's like I become a machine and the machine becomes a man. I talk to my cars, baby them, shout at them, praise them. I feel them live and breathe in my hands.

Cale Yarborough, American driver (Andrew Malkovich, *Sports Quotations*)

The Porsche, as I have always regarded it, is more than simply an automobile. It embodies my philosophy of freedom, of individual progression, serving mankind without burdening it.

Ferdinand Porsche (Alan Henry, *Driving Forces*)

CIRCUITS

Silverstone is tatty. It is Portakabin City in a sea of temporary scaffolding. To the telecamera it all looks chirpy; to the naked eye it's a tip.

Eddie Butler, journalist

When I get into the car at Silverstone, it is for everything except money.

Nigel Mansell

One of the earliest results of a Socialist Government is to deprive the motorist of one of the only two places in this country where long-distance, high-speed motoring events could be held and witnessed. Deplorable as such an action may be considered from a purely sporting viewpoint, it is even more remarkable as proof that uncoordinated planning leads to far worse results than unregulated private action.

Motor magazine, on the sale of Brooklands after the war (Richard Garrett, *The Motor Racing Story*)

Nigel Mansell and Silverstone: a combination so exciting that it should carry a health warning.

Nigel Mansell – *The Full Story by the Daily Express*

The acid test of a car is a road-course. Throughout the length and breadth of England there is no road-course. Thank God! sigh the beauty-lovers, the anti-litter societies, the institutions

6

for the Preservation of Rural Spots, and whenever the word speed is murmured, they rush up on to a high and lonely hill in their little shorts and open shirts, and setting their enormous banner in the ground, cry, 'No roadster shall pass this way!'

Sir Tim Birkin, *Full Throttle* (writing in the 1940s)

COMMENTATORS

We're now on the 73rd lap and the next one will be the 74th.

Murray Walker, during the 1992 Monaco Grand Prix

Certainly in the past three years, television has improved considerably. But I think the commentators are either not brave enough to give opinions, or they don't read the race correctly. Therefore, they do not give enough information to the viewers. If the commentary is not good then it doesn't matter how good the images are; the whole thing lacks interest and excitement. I'm not talking about anyone in particular. I'm just saying that, in general, the commentators don't do a good enough job.

Bernie Ecclestone

James has just nipped out to have a look at the far side of the circuit. (*see opposite*)

Euphemism used by Murray Walker during race commentaries with James Hunt who would leave the commentary box to smoke a joint

Nigel Mansell – the Man of the Race – the Man of the Day – the Man from the Isle of Man.

Murray Walker

I wouldn't like to be sitting in Alain Prost's shoes right now.

Barry Sheen

If they have any shillelaghs in Suzaka, they'll be playing them tonight.

Murray Walker, after Eddie Irvine's sixth place in his first Grand Prix

Your luck goes up and down like swings and roundabouts.

James Hunt

You can't see a digital clock because there isn't one.

Murray Walker

I make no apologies for their absence; I'm sorry they're not here.

Murray Walker

I do think the Europeans have had this attitude that no one can impregnate their superiority.

Jackie Stewart

He's obviously gone in for a wheel change. I say 'obviously' because I can't see it.

Murray Walker

He's watching us from hospital with his injured knee.

Murray Walker

I'd like to think I come across as a slightly over-the-top enthusiast. It is a very exciting sport after all.

Murray Walker

In his quieter moments he sounds as if his trousers are on fire.

Clive James, writer and broadcaster, on Murray Walker

Mansell is slowing it down, taking it easy. Oh no he isn't! It's a lap record.

Murray Walker

I don't make mistakes. I make prophecies which immediately turn out to be wrong. And I've done a lot of those, but I have no regrets and I make no apologies, because they're a reflection of enthusiasm and involvement, I like to think.

Murray Walker

It's not quite a curve, it's a straight actually

Murray Walker

Unless I'm very much mistaken . . . I am very much mistaken.

Slogan on T-shirts produced by the Murray Walker Fan Club

An Achilles heel for the McLaren team this year, and it's literally the heel because it's the gear box.

Murray Walker

And now the boot is on the other Schumacher.

Murray Walker

A strange experience. It all felt a bit unnatural, you feel like an actor. I've never had so much piss taken out of me in one weekend.

Derek Warwick, on his new role of TV commentator

The atmosphere is so tense you could cut it with a cricket stump.

Murray Walker

CONSTRUCTORS

Constructors are businessmen, not poets.

Jean-Marie Balestre

Every time the teams sit down and talk, it's very emotional. It's like school; everybody is screaming and then the teacher arrives and says 'Everybody, shut up!' This is what Max [Mosley] does.

Flavio Briatore

From a banking point of view, most racing teams are illiquid; they shouldn't be trading. They're all mad. To stay in the game, you know, you spend everything you have and then you hope you don't spend too much you don't have.

Eddie Jordan

Who needs a new team? A new entry is another one joining the scrabble to find budgets. It's a war.

Keith Wiggins, boss of Pacific Racing

You can't run a team by balancing the monthly figures. You have to stick your neck out. Risk losing it, but stick it out. Otherwise you have no place in F1.

Ron Dennis

I'm not trying to create a holiday camp environment, but team relationships are difficult things.

Ron Dennis

The thing that holds us all together is happiness.

J. J. Lehto, on the Benetton team

It was not difficult for me to reject McLaren's offer. I am happy at Benetton. We are building something special here and I want to see it completed.

Michael Schumacher

To run a Formula One team successfully is far more difficult and demanding than running a large multinational corporation. In a big company, you can always delegate your duties; you have an organisational chart that shows who reports to whom and why. You have minions and flunkeys to do your business. In Formula One you're just about naked. Each man on the team is naked. If a mechanic fails to put a bolt on properly, it's his responsibility when the inevitable shunt happens. He can't say he was following the orders of the second assistant from the left. He knew what his job was and he blew it.

Alan Jones, *Alan Jones – Driving Ambition*

The philosophy here is that we try to do all we can to inspire everybody who works for the company to do his part, to make his contribution to our common objective. This is winning, winning each and every race. Everything that distracts from this aim detracts from it.

Ron Dennis

DESIGN

Engine design is really a modern form of sculpture – a racing engine is a beautiful thing that actually has life.

   Graham Hill

Sticking to rigid engineering rules can be a great disadvantage, because that approach may steer you away from avenues of development that might otherwise be open. That's why experience and intuition, and all that seat-of-the-pants stuff, count for a hell of a lot.

   John Miles, engineer

I don't believe in blindly following what everyone else does just because it proves to be successful on one car. There's too much 'copy, copy, copy' in this business.

   John Barnard

Copy-cat engineering is a trait in many grand prix teams, but that will never put you in a competitive situation. You must go your own route. This is not an easy thing to achieve.

   Ron Dennis

The UK really is the Silicon Valley of world motor sport. It is the only place that exists with such a large technology base in one relatively small area. If you want any kind of specialist, high-tech components designed and made in quantities and within a timescale which any mainstream commercial engineering company would regard as lunatic, you virtually have to come here.

> Jonathan Ashman, marketing director of the RAC Motor Sports Association

The biggest influence on modern race car design and construction has been the US space programme.

> Dan Gurney (Rich Taylor, *Indy: Seventy-Five Years of Racing's Greatest Spectacle*)

Perhaps it is underestimated by some designers, but the ability of the guy to drive the car is a factor in winning races! The designer who doesn't take that into account is a fool. Just size alone isn't the only criteria, it is the comfort of the car; how many bits stick into his legs; how difficult is it to turn the wheel and change gear; does he hit his elbow? These are the sort of things that have an effect.

> John Barnard

You never look back and you never stop.

> Frank Williams, on car design

The machines have taken away the character and it is the character that sponsors and public are looking for. At the top you have a few characters of conflicting personality; the rest, without any good results, don't have any credibility. We must reduce costs so that we return to an era where the emphasis is on people, not computers.

> Ayrton Senna

You must think of all the problems that are liable to arise. Development is only necessary because of the ignorance of the designer, and since I don't want to appear more ignorant than is absolutely necessary, I try to get things right first time.

Keith Duckworth

I think that my main advantage is that I do not mind realising that I cannot fully understand most of the problems.

Keith Duckworth

Designing stunning cars is the only thing that fulfils me – it's like a war.

Colin Chapman

A lot of engineers just solve problems. I think there are ten solutions to every problem, and you shouldn't ever be satisfied with the first one. You work three, five, ten solutions, then you find one that has this particular merit in terms of simplicity, elegance, cost, refinement. When you've wrung it to death, and you can say, 'that's the essence', then you build it.

Colin Chapman

Spam in the can.

A phrase originally used to describe the early astronauts whose craft was controlled from earth. Now used to describe motor racing drivers in the light of increasing technology.

We're dealing with an art, not a science. An art because we don't really understand why. The answer may cost a lot, but it's there for the asking.

Derek Gardner, designer

17

Technology takes a lot from the driver. After the start, the race is for the computer, not the driver.

Nigel Mansell

It was a great privilege to be able to work for Ferrari for many years, particularly for Enzo Ferrari himself. That is an experience I wouldn't have missed for the world. But you know you do come to understand why the British are good at motor racing. There is an ease of operation, a common sense, which we are capable of within this industry in this country. It's nothing to do with money, nothing to do with facilities. It's simply that motor racing is much, much easier to do here in the UK somewhere to the north-west of London, than it is anywhere else in the world

Harvey Postlethwaite

Carburettor Valley

Name given by *Time* magazine to an area within a 150-mile radius of Heathrow Airport where the world's motor racing industry is based

We are in danger of introducing a breed of computerised dinosaur. We are facing a situation where the electronics may become more complicated than the engines.

Nobuhiko Kawamoto, president of Honda

Our sport is controlled, unfortunately, by computers. People don't understand we're small cogs in a big wheel. Fingers still slip, but the human element is being replaced by computer bugs, glitches and spikes.

Nigel Mansell

DESIGN

You are in an endless corridor, along which every door is closed. You want to get out but you can't. You have to find a solution. I find it sometimes in the night, sometimes as if in a dream. When I see a possibility, it is like a blinding light, like lightning. In my head I say, 'Why not a machine like this or that?' I become a thinking instrument, I guess at a concept, I formulate a theme.

Enzo Ferrari

F1 is special because it's a platform for the most sophisticated technique of motor sport, because it is extreme, at the far edge of innovation.

Keke Rosberg and Keith Botsford, *Keke – An Autobiography*

Engines are like sons: one settles down and studies and another signs cheques and is dissolute.

Enzo Ferrari (Gino Rancati, *Enzo Ferrari*)

DRIVERS

They are quite introverted, shy and intelligent, but on the whole they have few interests outside motor racing and a few other sports.

Berenice Krikler, psychiatrist

We are the test pilots of the road.

Stirling Moss

When I look fast, I'm not smooth and I am going slowly. And when I look slow, I am smooth and going fast.

Alain Prost

The layman cannot possibly know the feeling of a driver who has been through as much as I have, sitting today behind the wheel of a racer. It is a challenge to the soul and I feel it very deeply.

John Surtees

He operates in a continuum of impending disaster, for the race is one long emergency, one long red alert to all parts of his brain.

Angela Patmore, *Sportsmen Under Stress*

All a good tennis player needs is a pair of pumps and a racket. A good F1 driver needs £30 million worth of technology and a character that suits the marketing strategy of the sponsor.

Martin Brundle

You could almost say I was born with a spanner in my mouth.

Stirling Moss

People who are really good, or great, never really appreciate their own ability.

Jackie Stewart

Everything changes, but one thing is constant; a driver races to win. But so much has to do with preparation. If the car goes well, the driver is just another element. But when the car is a bad one, that is when the really good drivers, the strong ones, come to the fore. Just like life, motor racing favours those with character.

Juan Fangio

The only well-adjusted Formula One driver is Jackie Stewart. The rest are all a bit mad in some way. I suppose they need to be to take on what they do.

Dai Llewellyn

As a result of practice, which must be thorough, he should know exactly what he can do. He should know, to an inch, the most effective point for braking and acceleration. It is, in fact, almost a routine job.

Stirling Moss

Most drivers, to be honest, are thick. They go to meet Fred [Rogers – Jordan's business partner] and he takes them out for lunch and introduces them to some basic facts – like how to use a knife and fork.

Eddie Jordan

The true champion who shines is the one who people love to see, love to know, love to think about and to be with in their minds. In many ways we are a dream for people, not a reality.

Ayrton Senna

I think a lot of people race because of an inferiority complex. If you have one, you either give in to it or try to overcome it. I wanted to do something that other people couldn't do. I was invariably spinning off, although I did win at Brooklands once. There comes a time with every driver when they either kill themselves or get good.

Rob Walker

John Arlott once described Sir Jack Hobbs as 'Christlike'. I thought it was a bit over the top, but it describes Fangio.

Doug Nye, motoring historian

A driver mustn't have off days. He must always maintain the pressure.

Colin Chapman

A driver's life has two parts. One is how he behaves in his car, the other is how he behaves out of it.

Colin Chapman

I get on very well with my male colleagues on the track. I've learnt a lot from them. But, my God, how they hate you to do well or to win. And for no other reason than because you're a woman.

Divina Galica

Like a first-growth Mouton-Rothschild or a solo by Charlie Parker, his qualities are inaccessible and not instantly appreciated. Although they may demand a little time and application to discover, the effort is worthwhile.

Mike Doodson, *Nelson Piquet*

Contrary to what a lot of people write, I have no special talent for recognising drivers that are good. If they're quick, they're good.

> Ken Tyrrell

Once I have mastered the geography of the circuit the next stage follows naturally and usually quite quickly. This involves moulding myself into the elements and consciously refusing to compete against them. Instead of looking for landmarks I synchronise my mental picture of the circuit with the picture that is being received by my eyes and I keep these two pictures in synch as I increase my speed.

> Jackie Stewart

People want superstars and Niki is an obvious one. His accident gave him mystique, he came back from the dead.

> Ron Dennis, on Niki Lauda

Some drivers grow the fruit. Others come in and pick it.

> Nigel Mansell

I don't understand how 26 of the finest drivers can turn into a bunch of hooligans at the first bend.

> John Watson

Perhaps these men who drive racing cars to the extreme limits of adhesion are the gladiators of this century. They are all touched with romance, and terribly often they die in their battles with the machine. It is a little unclear whom they are fighting – the machine, certainly; each other, often; perhaps most of all themselves.

> J. R. L. Anderson, writer

DRIVERS

What is of primary importance is that they can win Grands Prix and hopefully be clever enough to put championships together. Secondly, they have to fit commercially. There are commercial pressures from partners and sponsors.

Frank Williams

I admire drivers very much because I always wanted to be a racing driver. Of course, they are a pain in the bum sometimes, a bit precocious, selfish, aggressive. That's what makes them. That's them. They've got to be mean inside.

Frank Williams

I don't stand for much nonsense from drivers, and I don't treat them like superstars. They are employees, here to do a job like everyone else.

Eddie Jordan

You have to choose a driver who has not only ability but promotability. In Formula One there are two businesses. There is the motor racing and then there is the commercial side. You can have the best drivers in the world but if they can't speak properly it's a bit of a downer. We thought choosing a female was the best option commercially – the bonus is that she can also drive.

Dennis Nursey, then managing director of Brabham, explaining the signing of Giovanna Amati

The driver is a vital component that must be kept in perfect adjustment just like any other part of the car.

Bobby Rahal, IndyCar driver (Rich Taylor, *Indy: Seventy-Five Years of Racing's Greatest Spectacle*)

Self-mocking humour and gallant gestures are part of another era, when drivers had private incomes and wore fighter-pilot moustaches. You can risk your life with a wry smile and a light quip but, when you are risking your backer's millions, it is only polite to act po-faced.

Simon Barnes, journalist

Why should I respect another driver? Respect is something I have for people who work with the poor in the Third World.

Eddie Irvine

Racing is a business today. The palmy amateur days of debonair, dashing drivers have gone. You have got to keep a cool, calculating head. You have to be a professional, there is no room for the characters of a few years ago – today's drivers are young, dedicated products of the scientific age.

Jim Clark, in 1964

There is no room in modern motor racing for unapproachable gods and supermen. You are simply selling your skill just like everybody else.

Guy Edwards

As a racing driver there are some things you have to go through, to cope with. Sometimes they are not human, yet you go through it and do them just because of the feelings that you get by driving, that you don't get in another profession. Some of the things are not pleasant, but in order to have some of the nice things, you have to face them.

Ayrton Senna

DRIVERS

Every driver in F1 is capable of driving to a level beyond comprehension. But not more than one or two have the intelligence to become world champion.

Pat Symonds, Michael Schumacher's racing engineer

There are too many old drivers in this sport. A few years ago a couple of drivers a year got killed and no one took any notice. It was a sort of natural culling.

Bernie Ecclestone

I live to do this, to be the best driver in the world, and when it is over, then I will be like other men.

Ayrton Senna

Winning a race isn't a big thrill. The thrill is going into the first corner on a long race, watching 20 cars drifting all around you; you've a full tank of petrol . . . and you can feel the back of the car sliding away.

Roy Salvadori, whose mother's maiden name was Ferrari

You could almost say I was born with a spanner in my mouth.

Stirling Moss

All racing drivers at a certain level are given a gift from God, a natural talent. The fellows who are very good, and turn out to be exceptional, exercise that talent to the fullest extent through management of the mind.

Jackie Stewart

The guy is as tough as nails. He's been there. Year after year. The damn machine's going to quit on him before he'll give in. He just keeps coming back. I mean, *tough*!

Buck Owens, Wyoming businessman, on A. J. Foyt

When you are on a winning streak, it's like being a star in a movie or on TV. But with a movie star you can carry on until you drop dead – with motor racing you are forced to get out before your time, because there is always someone desparately trying to jump into your driving seat.

Derek Bell

Every time a driver takes off, we write him off in our book. When he comes back it's a bonus.

Enzo Ferrari (Gerald Donaldson, *Gilles Villeneuve*)

The crowds loved him because he, of all the men out there, was so clearly working without a net.

Nigel Roebuck, journalist, on Gilles Villeneuve (ibid.)

In Formula One you're part of a racing stable and the number-one driver is the stud.

Didier Pironi (ibid.)

My pet peeve among drivers are the ones who can theorise all day but can't put any of their theory into practice. A lot of American drivers can talk their way around a track better than they can drive around one. I don't want to criticise them for each is doing what he thinks best, but Americans are simply more deeply into bullshit and technology. Give them a new car perfectly set up and they'll shove it through wind-tunnels and a graduate department at a university and have the car two seconds slower in no time.

Alan Jones, *Alan Jones – Driving Ambition*

The French tend to be their own worst enemies. Ligier, for instance, is a very good team; good drivers, good cars. But they will turn up at a track, do a handful of laps in super-quick times and then retire for a three-hour lunch to celebrate.

Alan Jones (ibid.)

When speed gets in the blood, one must drive to live.

Rudolf Caracciola (Andrew Malkovich, *Sports Quotations*)

Laugh if you like, but the Grand Prix stars of my era had more in common with Battle of Britain pilots than with today's racing heroes.

Stirling Moss and Mike Hailwood, *Racing and All That*

Someone equated racing drivers to light bulbs: you take one out and you put another one in.

John Watson (Christopher Hilton, *Alain Prost*)

You know, when you're in motor racing your relationship with the driver who's driving for you is very strong. The minute he stops it hardly exists. That's the way it is.

Teddy Mayer (ibid.)

As for sex, if you look at a driver's harness in the cockpit and realise how the belts squeeze all the blood out of your balls, I wouldn't describe the feeling as at all sexy.

Keke Rosberg and Keith Botsford, *Keke – An Autobiography*

You have to be hungry all the time. You can never be satisfied. A complacent driver is a retired driver.

Rusty Wallace, stock-car racer

Most people have got our image all wrong. We don't all sit around eating our Yorkie bars and chatting away on the CB.

Dick Pountain, truck racer

To be racing in this kind of competition, every driver has to have what we call a 'seat of the pants' feeling about the car. If you don't know enough to pull into the pits and have the car looked at when you think there may be a problem, you don't belong on the track in the first place.

Mark Donohue (Phil Berger and Larry Bortstein, *The Boys of Indy*)

On the track you are on your own with every man trying to beat the chap in front, and then after the race there is the inevitable party, with all the drivers and officials, mechanics and entrants, and as the evening develops the laughter gets louder, the jokes get bawdier, the horseplay gets horsier, and the people concerned forget whether they won or lost and settle in to letting their hair down and having a really good time.

Innes Ireland, *All Arms and Elbows* (1967)

I regard most of them as business men in overalls. I can't wait for the day when they begin to turn up at the track in striped trousers and bowler hats, carrying rolled umbrellas and briefcases.

Innes Ireland (ibid.)

He's got to be intelligent. Generally speaking, there are no thick world champions – never has been one. Of the current thirty-odd drivers, two or three, I suppose, are thick. But that's not a very nice expression, is it?

Ken Tyrrell (Tony Howard, *Countdown to a Grand Prix*)

People say that, knowing the risks, a race driver is a madman. They are not altogether wrong, except that deep down those risks are calculated ones. But the passion made us forget them.

Luigi Villoresi (Kevin Desmond, *The Man with Two Shadows*)

When I say I'm a racing driver, it's just as though I'd said, 'I eat children.'

Evelyn Mull, American racer, writing in the 1950s (Evelyn Mull, *Women in Sports Car Competition*)

You can't win. Being a woman you must be a poor driver or, if you're a good driver, you must be unfeminine.

Evelyn Mull (ibid.)

These prewar drivers who had survived the rigours of World War Two were real characters. Some terrific parties went on there, as well as frolics. They had taken the fuses out of the hotel lights, planted trees around the bar and Freddie Dixon had even broken up the piano. I remember that the local police came to quieten things down a bit and everyone promised to go to bed. But then the chaps poured petrol and benzol into the swimming pool and set it alight, and that meant calling out the fire brigade. Later, this same lot got hold of a pass key and as there were other people staying at the hotel apart from the race drivers, the practical jokers had a wonderful time of it. The hotel boasted quite a decent farmyard of its own, and before long hotel guests found geese, chickens and pigs in their bedrooms. At three o'clock in the morning the hotel was really a fun place to be in.

John Cooper, recalling a trip to race on the Isle of Man (John Cooper, *Grand Prix Carpetbagger*)

My first driver is the fastest driver.

Ken Tyrrell (Jean-Claude Halle, *François Cevert: A Contract with Death*)

One soon realises that there is no archetypal racing driver, and that the next World Champion could be that unemployed guy you see collecting the benefit – as in the case of Graham Hill – or else the cocky little kid down the road with the flash Austin Healey and the jaunty walk to match – like Jackie Stewart. The emergence of a World Champion racing driver is not the result of selective breeding, of tender or rich upbringing, or of opportunities served up on a silver plate, but rather the result of a strange chemistry, the ingredients of which exist in nearly all of us, but not in the correct proportions.

Graham Gauld, *Jim Clark – The Legend Lives On*

EMOTIONS

A driver cannot allow his feelings to show. I plug my brain into the car and go on automatic pilot.

Nigel Mansell

Emotion is a lovely privilege but it is one I cannot afford during a race. If another driver has a shunt in front of me I must take advantage of any situation that may arise. I am, as I say, completely detached.

Jackie Stewart

You can be aggressive, but you must remain emotionally cool. The more your emotions run you, the more you'll make mistakes.

Bobby Rahal, IndyCar driver (Rich Taylor, *Indy: Seventy-Five Years of Racing's Greatest Spectacle*)

Basically, my talent for overriding my emotions by staying detached and objective has served me well. There is really no point in having a complex about losing half an ear. Take a good look at yourself in the mirror; that's you, that's the way you are. And if people don't like you that way you might as well forget them. I even capitalised on my semi-baldness by signing with Parmalat to wear a cap with their name on it; even now I'm retired, that cap still has the same promotional value.

Niki Lauda, *To Hell and Back*

FAILURE

I feel ashamed of myself. It was as if I had done something
dirty, like being caught as a neighbourhood Peeping Tom.
I'd been robbed of my pride. It was so bad I was even afraid
to walk down the pit lane.

> John Watson, after failing to qualify for the 1980 Monaco Grand
> Prix

There is no room for failure. It's the quick and the dead.

> Bernie Ecclestone

Winning is an anti-climax and it is an embarrassment.
But losing really burns and that's what drives on most
sportsmen.

> Robin Herd

FEAR

Fear is a funny thing. Once you have a taste of it then you can't live without it. I need danger. There is nothing like the lure of forever cheating death.

David Purley

I don't believe a racing driver is necessarily a brave man, as much as a man who isn't afraid.

The Marquis de Portago (William Court, *Grand Prix Requiem*)

Yes, I get scared, we all get scared, but I get scared that something will happen to the car. It's the cars that break, not the drivers.

Jochen Rindt (ibid.)

Sometimes it's hollow-eyed scary. Sometimes when you come off the track and get out of the car you know how close you have been to not getting out of the car.

Perry McCarthy

Every time you go into the car, fear comes round you. It's a hell of emotion, danger. While you are doing it, something is telling you – I don't like this. I don't feel good, I don't feel comfortable. But after you have faced it, there is a great relief and you feel very calm. You are playing with strong emotions all the time.

Ayrton Senna

FERRARI

I feel alone after a life crowded by so many events and almost
guilty of having survived.

Enzo Ferrari

Driving for Ferrari is like driving for the Pope.

Nigel Mansell

I wish the Pope would make you a cardinal, Enzo.
Why a cardinal?
Because then we would only have to kiss your ring.

Conversation between an executive and Enzo Ferrari

. . . a modern Saturn who continues to devour his children.

L'Osservatore Romano, the Vatican newspaper, on Enzo Ferrari

The team's famous prancing horse symbol has been looking
as sick as a Cleethorpes donkey recently

Stan Piecha, journalist

Today we celebrate the Resurrection of Christ – and also of
Ferrari.

The local priest at Maranello, after Nigel Mansell won his first race
for Ferrari

I never eat out until about three days after a race. If we've done well I get pestered and if we've not done well I don't get served.

Harvey Postlethwaite, on his time at Ferrari

Ferrari is the greatest name in motor sport and I deem it a privilege to be able to drive for them.

Nigel Mansell

For us F1 is not a cost but a traditional expenditure.

Luca di Montezemolo, president of Ferrari

I was a young bloke on the way up and two other teams had been after me but the great Commendatore (the patriarch Enzo Ferrari) had asked for me, a little farm lad from Sussex . . . But the cars were so slow at that time. It was the greatest experience of my life as well as, ultimately, the biggest disappointment. Now they've got it all together again, I honestly still get a real thrill when Ferrari win today, nearly 20 years later.

Derek Bell

Well, well, young man, how much do you need to be content?

Supposedly Enzo Ferrari's first words to Gilles Villeneuve (Gerald Donaldson, *Gilles Villeneuve*)

Crisis is almost the normal state at Ferrari. When you win there is a crisis of optimism.

Alain Prost (Christopher Hilton, *Alain Prost*)

He's the most incredible man I have ever met and I have known a lot of people. He's a legend, he's like Winston Churchill. People will always talk about him and I hope he lives 200 years.

Bernie Ecclestone (Gino Rancati, *Enzo Ferrari*)

There was always furore at Ferrari – from Fangio to Alboreto.

Niki Lauda, *To Hell and Back*

I am not much of a hand at 'historical method' and the cults of legend. For me Enzo Ferrari was just the Chief of my racing team, and I always treated him with respect, but straightforwardly.

Niki Lauda, *For the Record: My Years with Ferrari*

As I get older I have much more understanding of, and admiration for, the man than I ever did when I was driving for him because I can identify much more with what he was. Ferrari had a clear vision of what he wanted to pursue and he just did it. Enzo Ferrari was a tough man, very tough, and totally dedicated to his life's work.

Phil Hill

FORMULA ONE

When I was racing stock cars, Grand Prix racing seemed so remote, such a world away, that I did not think in terms of progressing to circuit racing one day. To be honest, in stock-car racing we tended to view Grand Prix drivers as, well, poofters. Ours was the real motor sport.

Derek Warwick

When you start off as a driver, it is a sport; but when you get into Formula One, it suddenly becomes a job.

Alain Prost

[It is] like going to war. If you get blown away in the first race, you come back here to the factory and work your nuts off for two weeks and fight to the death for the next race. It was like that in the war. They never stopped developing the Spitfire. They had to do it. The pressure was on.

Frank Williams

Formula One is a mix of power, speed, human beings fighting together. Noise and lifestyle, that is what Formula One is about.

Flavio Briatore

If you want prosciutto, you go to Italy. If you want champagne, you go to France. For Formula One, you come to England.

Flavio Briatore

Grand Prix motor racing viewed from the outside has all the small village jealousies of the Archers.

Ian Wooldridge

The principle of Grand Prix racing for me has not changed at all – it was always difficult and competitive. Even the people are almost the same except that we all seem to have more wrinkles.

Niki Lauda, after his return to Formula One

Formula One is a diabolical collision of all that is both desirable and undesirable about humanity. Because it is capital-intensive (its huge funding is paid up-front rather than in prize money) and because it is romantic and colourful and dangerous and noisy it attracts people of that kind – car-dealers, gamblers and the nouveau-riche.

Profile in *The Observer*

Formula One and the Indianapolis 500 have a mutual disrespect for each other.

Robin Herd, chairman of March Engineering

I know F1 is the pinnacle of technology and all that but it is also entertainment.

Flavio Briatore

In one sense, grand prix racing is like a banana republic – one revolution after another.

Tony Howard, *Countdown to a Grand Prix*

FORMULA ONE

The only certainty in Grand Prix racing is that there are no certainties. The Ides of March plotters could take lessons from Formula One.

Nigel Mansell – The Full Story by the Daily Express

Formula One is a terrible thing, it can really hurt, hurt you bad mentally and screw you up bad. There are very few straight people in it.

Tommy Byrne (Christopher Hilton, *Gerhard Berger: The Human Face of Formula One*)

There is nothing mysterious or magical about Formula One – everything is logical and everything has an explanation.

Alain Prost, *Life in the Fast Lane*

FRIENDS

I do not know what a friend is. In motor racing you have lots of friends when you win. You have fewer friends when you lose. The friends you have when you lose are only there because they think you will win again.

Niki Lauda

Most of my friends are from five to ten years ago. I don't have new friends though I get on with the young people in Formula One.

Ayrton Senna

It's very difficult to have a relationship with a fellow competitor 'cos the next thing you're doing is touching wheels at 200 mph.

Derek Warwick

It may seem strange to the outside world, but we don't mix all that much, as drivers. We belong to the same world and we know each other's foibles, qualities and defects, but it's largely limited to that. The rivalry is perhaps too intense for any real camaraderie. If I play backgammon with another driver, it's to beat him and put him off his feed.

Alan Jones, *Alan Jones – Driving Ambition*

You can be friendly, but it's hard to be friends.

Peter Revson, *Speed With Style*

FRIENDS

I know that, in Formula One, there can be no real relationships or friendships, except maybe, between a front-runner and a back-marker.

Michael Schumacher

FUEL

I think it's optimistic to suggest we won't have any fires. The refuelling equipment seems well designed, but the fact remains that you're handling a flammable liquid in a situation of stress, and it's inevitable that mistakes will be made. The real question is, when an accident happens is it going to be controllable?

Ron Dennis

The real absurdity is that refuelling has been introduced for no reason other than to provide spectacle for the TV cameras and perhaps enliven a dull race.

Nigel Roebuck, journalist

It should be safe. If aircraft can be refuelled at 30,000 feet, we should be able to do it.

Gerhard Berger

I told the team that if they did not want to do refuelling we wouldn't. We would lose the World Championship but I said I didn't care. I said that because I was the one who took all those telephone calls in Germany from mothers, wives, girlfriends, sons and daughters who had just seen their men burning.

Flavio Briatore

FUEL

I'm not keen on the idea of someone trying to chuck 100 litres of fuel down the back of my neck. In all this there is a risk of a few spillages.

Damon Hill

INDYCAR

All I had to do is keep turning left.

George Robson, after winning in 1946

There's no secret. You just press the accelerator to the floor and steer left.

Bill Vukovich

The Indy 500 has more pressure than any other event in racing. You feel like a balloon. Every day they put more pressure in. It's very difficult to deal with so much pressure.

Emerson Fittipaldi (Rich Taylor, *Indy: Seventy-Five Years of Racing's Greatest Spectacle*)

It was a great race. Hell to be out there and hell to be part of but a great race.

Nigel Mansell, after his first Indy 500

The Indianapolis 500 is really a great British motor race.

Colin Wilson, communications manager of the RAC Motor Sports Association, citing the fact that most chassis and engines used in the 1993 Indy 500 were designed and built in Britain

I don't think I've really absorbed it yet. I know I was grinning from ear to ear in my cool-off lap.

Janet Guthrie, a physicist, after becoming the first woman to qualify for the Indy

There's no question the Indianapolis 500 is the biggest race in the world, period, over and above Formula One. From a spectator's point of view and from a sponsor's point of view IndyCar racing has a lot to offer.

Nigel Mansell

The first few laps were hell.

Nigel Mansell, on his first Indy 500

The slaughter that marked the 1973 Indianapolis cannot be categorised as accidental deaths. What happened on the infamous speedway has come to be a routine form of homicide. In 57 years of racing in Indianapolis there has not been a year without a serious accident. Furthermore, the annual mayhem at Indianapolis only encourages it elsewhere. Such lethal circuses are in no sense justified by their morbid popularity. The prime issue is that of public safety and of public morality (concern for human life). But there are important secondary issues also, notably the wasteful consumption of fuel at a time of shortages which threaten to curtail the legitimate use of automobiles and aircraft. Such intolerable waste – along with the glorification of murderous speed – in the face of worsening energy crisis is comparable to the public burning of food at a time of famine. The 1973 débâcle at Indianapolis deserves to be turned into the tombstone and epitaph of a savage aberration in the world of sport.

New York Times

I love Indianapolis. It's ecstasy for me.

Lyn St James, IndyCar driver

It is a universal truth that most people, even non-sports followers, have some idea of what the Indianapolis 500 is. And it is another universal truth that most people have no idea where to find Indianapolis on the map. It is a city almost wholly defined by a single annual event; beyond that, it has practically no international profile at all.

Kate Battersby, sports writer

Indianapolis; it would be fine without the Americans.

Jim Clark (Graham Gauld, *Jim Clark: The Legend Lives On*)

As a series it's a total shambles. It's like rent-a-car racing or having a showbiz wrestler up against a superbly fit boxer.

Bernie Ecclestone

Formula One today is politics, fighting and aggravation all the time. IndyCar racing is like a big happy family having a good time together every weekend. IndyCar racing is a sport and a business; Grand Prix has become only business. Crazy business.

Emerson Fittipaldi (Rich Taylor, *Indy: Seventy-Five Years of Racing's Greatest Spectacle*)

We send the old British drivers over to IndyCar racing.

Martin Brundle, asked if he fancied joining Nigel Mansell

It's a New Year, a new life and Formula One is history.

Nigel Mansell, on his way to IndyCar

INDYCAR

It's not my fault I will be in America. Frank Williams, Renault and the French government must be blamed for that.

Nigel Mansell

There is no question. I'm a marked man. Everybody and his dog wants to beat me.

Nigel Mansell, preparing for his IndyCar début

Why did they let this guy go? If I had been Frank Williams I'd 'a killed to keep him.

Carl Haas, partner of the Newman Haas Racing team, on Nigel Mansell

MECHANICS

You'll notice that most of the mechanics hardly ever touch the engine. They used to be called grease monkeys but they're keyboard monkeys now. (*see opposite*)

Nigel Mansell

Mechanics are the link that connects drivers to either happiness or death. When you leave the pits to start a race, you know you may never come back. You have to trust these guys.

Niki Lauda

Imola is the most crowded race of the year. Our pits are full of famous people and Fiat top brass. It gets so bad we're handing tools to each other through photographer's legs and round people who want Nigel [Mansell]'s autograph. It's not easy to work like this, but we're used to it. Everybody wants to touch the car, to stroke it. We have to keep calm.

Umberto Benassi, chief mechanic at Ferrari

On the eve of the race, one or more mechanics sleep beside the car, guarding it as a dragon a fairy princess, starting up at every sound. The morning of the race dawns, there is a last frantic inspection, and they stand back, each man represented by some part of the engine or body, and survey their child in silence. After that it is rudely seized from them by the driver, and they are compelled to watch it passively

from the pits, recognising from its tone, even when far away, whether they are to be rewarded or not. There is little they can do, once it is out of their hands; they are helpless after being indispensable.

Sir Tim Birkin, *Full Throttle*

THE MEDIA

They don't understand me and I don't understand them.

Nigel Mansell, on his relationship with the Italian media

The worst bit about racing is when you get out of the car. Journalists push you around, shove microphones under your face, they're all hot and sweaty, and all you feel like doing is having a drink and breathing fresh air.

Nelson Piquet

If they don't write muck in the story then someone else writes muck in the headline.

Johnny Dumfries, then the Earl of Dumfries, now the Marquess of Bute

I think the most important thing if you want to keep going in motor racing is never to read anything. If you read bad things that people write, or you think maybe people are speaking bad things about you, you go and fight all the little details you should not fight – and then you have to stop Formula One. So first, I never read anything. Second, I am a friend of everybody. Anybody write bad things about me, next day I am talking to him, no problems. I don't make enemies.

Nelson Piquet

I don't like to see sensational writing about the sport.

Graham Hill

I've had reporters phone me at 3 o'clock in the morning many times, often for quite a trivial reason. I've had reporters call me on the radio at 4 a.m. in Bangkok to take a call from London – and in Bangkok you just don't pick up the telephone, you have to go to the central post office to answer.

Stirling Moss

I sympathise with the Italian crowds – they treat racing like a religion, get very passionate, and are fed a complete load of rubbish by their press.

James Hunt (Jonathon Green and Don Atyeo, *The Book of Sports Quotes*)

Sometimes the attention is a pain in the neck, but you've got to put it into perspective; if I weren't where I am, they wouldn't be there, but if they weren't there, I wouldn't be where I am.

Mario Andretti (ibid.)

MONEY

We all want all the money we can get – not just for its own sake but because it is the measure of your success. If one driver is getting £1.5 million a year, then it's everyone's ambition to be a £1.5 million driver. It shows what you are. But it is not the money that brings you to the track. Money doesn't make you take impossible risks. But when people get killed, I feel we are worth the money. With 30 per cent of fatal accidents, I think, well, I would have been able to drive out of that one. But with the other 70 per cent, I know I would have absolutely no chance. Every driver must admit that. And I think of the money and say, well I *deserve* this.

Jonathan Palmer

Whatever salary any grand prix driver in the world gets, it is not enough money because he risks something more valuable than money – his life. I know what professional golfers or tennis players get. They're not risking anything and they get far more than us.

Nigel Mansell

Money has never been important except in that it reflects my ability.

Ayton Senna

We have a way of describing the financial boys at Lotus.

They are not there to join in the game, they're there to keep the score.

Colin Chapman

If a man drives from passion, neither the money nor the risk count; if a man drives as his business, it is right that he should value his life at what he considers a fair price.

Enzo Ferrari

Money never interested me as much as the driving, so when I discovered that someone would actually pay you for doing what you love best, that was it. Do you know, old boy, that I can make as much money in a morning these days signing limited editions of books and mementoes as I did when I won the European Grand Prix at Nurburgring in 1961. I got £600 for that and I was the happiest man on earth.

Stirling Moss

I've got too much money and I just had to get rid of it.

Frank Williams; explaining why he asked Nigel Mansell to rejoin his team

I have never forgotten what Ken Tyrrell said when I was trying to squeeze money from him in my first season: 'Son, you don't earn a penny because what you do is dangerous. You earn plenty because you are fast.' I have built my own philosophy on that.

Martin Brundle

What we do is fairly dangerous and that's why I feel we should make as much money as we can.

Peter Revson

It's not about the money. That's just the barometer.

Martin Brundle

Nigel Mansell's fans have taken to sending letters to Frank Williams, enclosing £10 notes to enable him to meet the financial demands of Britain's world motor racing champion.

Report in *The Daily Telegraph*

If the money disappeared overnight, I would still be in racing because I love it. The entrepreneurs would be gone.

Gilles Villeneuve (Gerald Donaldson, *Gilles Villeneuve*)

The fact is, we're all whores, aren't we? If the money's right we'll turn up anywhere and do our stuff.

Keke Rosberg

Not many of today's drivers have charisma. And the fastest race some of them have is the race to the bank.

Louis Stanley

Let's talk about Mansell. Somebody must love him. He comes back in France, according to the press, for £1m. And he'll get £3m for the last three races. In France there were 72 laps and he did 46 and he was lying, until those two cars shunted each other, a bad fifth. That's more than £21,000 for each of those laps, and he didn't have the courtesy to wait until the end to congratulate the winner. The payment is obscene. It's the tail wagging the dog.

Louis Stanley

Today all is commerce and cold blood. Do I approve or disapprove? I don't do either. I recognise things the way they are.

Alan Jones, *Alan Jones – Driving Ambition*

NEEDLE

He is always complaining.

Ayrton Senna, on Nigel Mansell

People hang on his every word and he thinks he is a superstar.
In fact, he is just a lot richer and a bit quicker than he was
four years ago when he joined us.

Frank Williams, on Nigel Mansell

If all his old girlfriends buy it, it'll be a bestseller.

Hot Rod Hundley's former wife, on his autobiography (*Sports Shorts*)

In one year I travelled 450,000 miles by air. That's 18½ times
around the world or once around Howard Cosell's head.

Jackie Stewart, on US sports broadcaster Howard Cosell (*Sports Shorts*)

When I saw he was going to punch me I thought, okay here's
a few quid coming my way. I don't care who he is or what he
says. He doesn't worry me.

Eddie Irvine, after being punched by Ayrton Senna following an
altercation during the 1993 Japanese Grand Prix

59

The São Paulo taxi driver.

Nelson Piquet, on Ayrton Senna

I didn't call Nigel a blockhead, but I did say he was stupid when he should have won the championship in 1986.

Nelson Piquet

So what is Ayrton going to do? Fix me with a Vulcan mind grip or something?

Damon Hill, responding to questions about how he would get on with Ayrton Senna as a team-mate

What a start to my Grand Prix career. I get punched by Senna in my first race, crash in my second, destroy four cars in my third and get banned from my fourth. People are going to think I'm some kind of nutter.

Eddie Irvine

Brilliant in the car, but a pain in the backside out of it.

Frank Williams, on Nigel Mansell

When a man holds you round the throat I do not think he has come to apologise.

Ayrton Senna, after an altercation with Nigel Mansell

This is probably what you get when you have one man who believes in God and another who believes he is God.

A member of the McLaren team, on the row between Ayrton Senna and Jean-Marie Balestre, the president of Fisa, after Senna criticised the organisation

What do you have to do for people to believe that you are any good? Last weekend I beat Mansell for pole position, and the year before in France I beat Prost for pole. Then in the race I came closer than anyone all year to beating Schumacher. And all I read is that my job is in jeopardy. It's not. I'm second in the championship. I've come here to beat Schumacher and turn the championship round. I have never heard such a load of bollocks as I've heard this week. I'm very pissed off.

Damon Hill, reacting to reports that his job is under threat

Damon's gone nuts.

How *The Sun* reported the issue

The Era of Mr Nasty
Manners makyth man, as any Wykehamist will tell you. But make him what? In the estimation of Mr Damon Hill, a racing driver taunted by the press, they make him a pushover. 'I don't get any credit for being polite and diplomatic,' he fumed in the preparation for tomorrow's British Grand Prix, 'so I'm going to ditch that tack. It's not got me anywhere.'
   Thousands of small boys who pin pictures of Mr Hill on their bedroom walls, or who sit hugged over imaginary steering wheels while watching his exploits on television, will be deeply affected by this statement. Yobbery is given another sanction, and once more it is sport that sets the poor example. Soccer went west long ago; cricket has now more than its share of oiks. But one had always felt, notwithstanding the ignoble whingeing of Mr Nigel Mansell, that motor racing still set a premium on gentility

61

off the track. One clung to fond memories of young men with cravats under their overalls tinkering of a morning in their mews garages, before taking the motor off to do battle at Brooklands or Silverstone. But those days are no more.

The wider philosophical point made by Mr Hill bears some scrutiny. The history of the world is not, as Carlyle said, the biography of great men, but the biography of nasty ones. One is reminded of the late President Nixon, defeated for the Governorship of California in 1962, scornfully and bitterly bidding farewell to the press by telling them that 'you won't have Dick Nixon to kick around any more'. Six years after turning nasty Mr Nixon became president.

The two most offensive men of our century, Adolf Hitler and Joe Stalin, managed 41 years in office between them, and so vile was the one that it took the inspirational loathsomeness of the other to help remove him. Both benefited from the principle of *oderint dum metuant* – let them hate so long as they fear – knowing that their vileness in enforcing their will was so stygian that few would dare to impede them.

The British, in particular, are bad when it comes to dealing with unpleasant people. We prefer not to cause a scene when someone else behaves badly, and so we tend to indulge them. Therefore, miscreants appear to get away with it. The meek may well inherit the earth, but there are no signs that the will is about to be read. We also, with our sympathy for the underdog, tend to feel comfortable with those who do not rampage and bluster, while distrusting and despising those who get their way by force of will. That, though, is a sympton of the British disease, of our national decline; a tad more ruthlessness in the past 50 years and we might not be where we are today.

Mr Hill (to mix our sports, if not our metaphors) tried to play the game by the laws of cricket, and could not win. The small boys who copy him will no doubt prove a trial to their parents, but they might at least have a bright future.

Very leading article in *The Daily Telegraph*

NEEDLE

He used us and I hope we don't see him again. He must think there's a big sign in the pit lane saying 'public convenience'.

Bernie Ecclestone, on Alain Prost's second retirement

I think I have enough experience to know what I am talking about – remember, I have won the world championship twice – Nigel has lost it once.

Nelson Piquet, on his then team-mate at Williams, Nigel Mansell

He'll be more of a chauffeur making sure the car does the work for him. I'm a better and far more courageous driver than he'll be if he's in Formula One for a lifetime or another ten years.

Nigel Mansell, on Alain Prost

Mosley is showing pure hatred of Germans with his actions. He only wants Damon Hill to advance.

A German racing fan, on Max Mosley after Michael Schumacher was banned for two races for ignoring a black flag at Silverstone

We're so furious we'll beat Mosley to a pulp if we get hold of him.

Hans Meier, German racing fan, on the same issue

If he has not had any lessons in self-defence, he should take some.

Nigel Mansell's advice to Damon Hill on how to approach his new team-mate Ayrton Senna

It's good, because Williams needs a name and so does F1. It will be nice to shoot him down.

Eddie Irvine, on Nigel Mansell's return from IndyCar

The only reason I would have wanted to stay in the sport was to blow Alain Prost away. To settle the score with him and prove who really is the best driver.

> Nigel Mansell, on retirement from Formula One and his replacement at Williams by Alain Prost

You know, the best situation in Australia that time would have been Prost in front, Keke second, me third and Nigel fourth. Nigel just needed third place to be champion, so I could have called the pits by radio and said, 'Hey, get on to Nigel and ask him how much he will pay to let him pass. Tell him it's £250,000 for him to win the championship.' I would have negotiated for sure. And if he had agreed, I would probably have changed my mind.

> Nelson Piquet, on the final race of the 1986 season during which Nigel Mansell crashed after a burst tyre (Mike Doodson, *Nelson Piquet*)

You've got a delay of two hours. No more priorities, no more VIP treatment. You left Ferrari, you bastard.

> An air-traffic controller to Niki Lauda as he attempted to leave Bologna airport after announcing he had left Ferrari (Niki Lauda, *For the Record: My Years With Ferrari*)

Lauda is worse than Judas. He sells himself for thirty sausages to our rivals.

> Enzo Ferrari, on the same episode (ibid.)

Any compromise is better than a successful lawsuit.

> Enzo Levi, for many years Ferrari's lawyer (Brock Yates, *Enzo Ferrari*)

NEEDLE

[Eddie] Irvine's three race suspension at the beginning of the year was far too short. His brain has obviously been removed and it is about time that his licence is too.

Peter Collins, Lotus boss, after Eddie Irvine crashed into Lotus's Johnny Herbert at the start of the 1994 Italian Grand Prix

[Damon] Hill has never been a number one driver. David Coulthard was quicker than him after three races. I don't have as much respect for him as I do for other drivers. I didn't expect him to stand up for me, but I didn't expect him to make it worse. He seemed the English gentleman, but when you are in trouble you get to know people.

Michael Schumacher

I have to say that I did make some comments this year about Damon [Hill], that I didn't have the respect for him that I maybe had for someone else. But I have to admit I was wrong. What he has done in the last two races in particular and what he must have done before has been a proper and a fantastic job. He has been a great rival and I must say 'sorry' for what I said.

Michael Schumacher

65

NICKNAMES

Little Godfather   Bernie Ecclestone

Hunt the Shunt   James Hunt

The Professor   Alain Prost

Derek the Cool   Derek Warwick

The Romford Flyer   Johnny Herbert

Muddy Talker   Murray Walker

Walker the Talker   Murray Walker

Il Mantovano Volante (The Flying Mantuan) Tazio Nuvolari

Il Maestro (The Master) Tazio Nuvolari

The Flying Doctor   Jonathan Palmer (who is a doctor)

The Fastest Medicine   Jonathan Palmer

Daredevil Divi   Divina Galica

The Tadpole   Alain Prost

Pick-up Piquet   Nelson Piquet

The Flying Scotsman   Jackie Stewart

Il Leone (The Lion)   Italian fans' nickname for Nigel Mansell

Andrea de Crasheris   Andrea de Cesaris

The Flying Dentist   Tony Brooks

The Black Prince   Emerson Fittipaldi

Chueco (Bandy Legs)   Juan Fangio

Harry   The nickname given to Ayrton Senna by his workmates who had difficulty pronouncing his Christian name when he first came to England.

True Brit   Nigel Mansell

Uncle Ken   Ken Tyrrell

The Philosopher   Ayrton Senna

The Belting Earl   Johnny Dumfries (then the Earl of Dumfries, now the Marquess of Bute)

Racer Chasers   Formula One groupies

The Madman   Ayrton Senna

The Track Brat   Ayrton Senna

The Bear   Denny Hulme

Son of the Devil   Tazio Nuvolari

The Great Little Man   Tazio Nuvolari

The Red Devil   Camille Jenatzy

The Wild Boar of the Ardennes   Raymond Sommer

Fast Eddie   Eddie Jordan

Little Rubens   Rubens Barrichello

Black Jack   Sir Jack Brabham

Tigress of Turin   Lella Lombardi

Jonah   John Watson

Miss Piaggios   Groupies

Gelignite Jack   Jack Murray (Australian driver)

The Lion Killer   Junior Johnson (American stock-car racer)

Little David   Junior Johnson

Fireball Roberts   Glenn Roberts (American stock-car racer)

Air Canada   Gilles Villeneuve

The Pilot   Gilles Villeneuve

The Golden Tortoise   Tazio Nuvolari

The Flying Scotsman   Jim Clark

The Rat   Niki Lauda

A gorilla   A driver lacking finesse.

The Monza Gorilla   Vittorio Brambilla

Calmer Palmer   Jonathan Palmer (since he became a commentator with Murray Walker)

The Racing Granny   Laine Daff (truck racer)

Meat Man Mel   Mel Lindsey (truck racer)

Queen of the Ice   Nancy Mitchell (rally driver in the fifties)

The Pope of the North   Enzo Ferrari

Captain Nice   Mark Donohue

Tough Tony   A. J. Foyt

The Rainmaster   Rudolf Caracciola

Nebelmeister (The Fog Master)   Bernd Rosemeyer

The Farnham Flyer   Mike Hawthorn

NOSTALGIA

Grand Prix motor racing is like *Punch*. It is never as good as it was.

Maxwell Boyd

Most of the personality has vanished from motor racing. You can pick out a driver only by the colour of his car or the motif on his crash helmet. They all look the same, they all drive the same.

Innes Ireland

The spirit of all sport has changed in 50 years, but none of them has deteriorated so much as Formula One racing. When I drove before the war all the teams – Alfa Romeo, Auto Union, Mercedes and Maserati – took it very seriously. But that didn't stop us being friends before and after a Grand Prix. It was a tradition that the winning driver would buy dinner for all his rivals after the race. I doubt if you would see Senna, Prost and Mansell even take a cup of coffee together.

Huschke von Hanstein

The days we enjoyed in motor racing were totally different from that degrading business when Nigel Mansell and Frank Williams washed their dirty linen in public. I think the whole episode has been horrendous.

Innes Ireland

There was a different atmosphere in motor racing just after the war. Most of us had just done six years of fighting, and having survived that we felt like letting off a bit of steam. And there was no better way as far as I was concerned than to be in a fast car going full tilt at a corner. We did it for the love of it, not to make money, that's the big difference with today. There was no television, no hype, very little sponsorship. It was a much more human sport in those days. We all looked out for each other. Because it wasn't a big money-making thing there was far more cooperation between rivals.

Duncan Hamilton

I think that's why there is so much more camaraderie among the men of my generation. In the '50s, on average, three top-line drivers were killed every year. We all went to far too many funerals. But that sense of being in the front line drew us all together.

Tony Brooks

I don't want to look back. People, mostly of my age bracket, say 'It's not like it was'. I think it's *exactly* like it was. Yes, of course there's more money now; a lot more control and organisation. But the *racing* is just the same . . . It was competitive then, and it's the same now. It's just as difficult to win races today – and it doesn't matter how big your budget is.

Ken Tyrrell

It was the best of times. There was so much more romance to life then than now. The places we travelled to, the people we met, the comradeship of the drivers, the exhilaration of the race . . . it was genuine fun. You know, at my first wedding six of the ushers were racing drivers. You'd never get that now. I met King Hussein, Jimmy Stewart, David Niven, Fidel Castro, the old King and Queen and some cracking birds. President Peron of Argentina gave me his handkerchief (nice one, too) when he saw me mopping my brow with an oily rag.

Stirling Moss

Now it's all different. Pretty girls are no longer allowed anywhere near the pit road. Wives and girls can't possibly enjoy themselves at Silverstone – all they seem to do is sit around and puff cigarettes. There's not even an after-race bash. In our day it used to be a condition of entry to attend prize-giving parties. Now any celebration happens on the rostrum in front of a very select few.

Bette Hill, widow of Graham Hill

As you have been reading about my rivals in racing, perhaps it might be of interest to let you have some idea of my personal relationship with them. My most important rivals became great friends of mine. Once we had climbed out of our cockpits, we just forgot all rivalry, and enjoyed talking to one another about the whole thing. Of course every driver tried his best in a race to beat each other, but when it was over it was done with that particular race, and the next race had to be planned anew.

Prince Bira, *Bits and Pieces* (1942)

Gone are the days when you could get four laps for a quid.

Graham Hill, *Life at the Limit*

Today, it's very namby-pamby stuff, kindergarten type of fun. There are no really riotous times such as we used to have. Everybody seems to be frightened of making merry as racing men once did.

Innes Ireland, *All Arms and Elbows*

THE POWERS THAT BE

I know that in the past the Constructors' Association has been likened to the Mafia and people have even called me the Godfather, but that's just not true. I wish I was a Godfather. They have millions of pounds in jets instead of railway trains like me. Believe me, if I were a Godfather I would not be getting involved in wrangles over racing cars roaring around a circuit.

Bernie Ecclestone

It's an Anglo-Saxon takeover.

Jean-Marie Balestre, after failing to be re-elected as president of Fisa

Fisa is my child. You are necessarily motivated to look after your child. I am very sentimental. And I have a great affection for the people who risk their lives.

Jean-Marie Balestre

It is never quite clear whether the people with bodyguards are simply being sensible, or whether they are in a terminal stage of egomania. However, it has been suggested that Jean-Marie Balestre has long since ceased to find this a useful distinction.

Simon Barnes, journalist, on Jean-Marie Balestre

PRESSURE

The last two or three years have been difficult financially, but if you're British you're supposed to overcome difficult periods.

Ken Tyrrell

I have not been relaxed for 30 years.

Alain Prost

It's bloody hard. The only thing that makes it easier is that you knew it was going to be hard. People expect you to go tits up. You have to show them that you are fighting on.

Nick Wirth, founder of Simtek

Pressure comes from within rather than from other people. And if pressure comes from other people it's how you deal with it.

David Coulthard

Pressure is something that builds when you're losing control.

David Coulthard

Pressure comes only when you have doubts about what you're doing, when you cannot see a way ahead. I do not worry about imponderables, about the word 'if'.

Ayrton Senna

It's all pressure, constant pressure. I don't react to pressure on the circuit because that's a closed world, but when I get out of the car the pressure is all over me again. On the track I can drive better if I'm pushed; but the outside weighs in on me. It's the people who think they own you, it's not having a body or a soul of your own.

Nelson Piquet

There's much more tension and electrification in snooker as a sport than in any other kind, even motor racing.

John Pulman, snooker player (Jonathon Green and Don Atyeo, *The Book of Sports Quotes*)

Whatever you may do in this sport, you're a bum unless you keep doing it. That's the pressure. It's a long way down, and you don't want to fall off. You don't ever want to hit bottom because it's no fun down there. That's what scares me actually. Not dying. Losing.

Al Unser (Phil Berger and Larry Bortstein, *The Boys of Indy*)

Auto racing is more demanding than most other sports. There's the concentration factor. I don't care what sport you pick out. You concentrate for a few minutes, an inning, a round, whatever it is. We have to concentrate for hours sometimes. We're travelling three hundred feet a second. If you forget yourself for a second, you're three hundred feet in the wall.

Wally Dallenbach, IndyCar driver (ibid.)

PROBLEMS

Excitement is a racing driver's biggest problem. It can deteriorate a man's performance more than anything.

Jackie Stewart

If you want to achieve your dreams, you've got to take chances. I haven't been able to keep up payments on the house so we've got to move out. We're hoping to move in with friends . . . There has been real pressure just to survive. Paying the shopping bills has sometimes been a problem and as for the electricity bills – don't ask. A few weeks ago I reached my lowest point because of the debts and repossession.

Perry McCarthy

Motor racing has always been the big goal in Perry's life and despite the setbacks he has always remained the eternal optimist. He deserves success.

Karen McCarthy, on her husband

As well as everything else, there was this lizard in the car. I kept trying to reach it to put it out of the car, but it kept getting away from me. It was still there at the end of practice.

Ronnie Peterson on unexpected difficulties during practice at Monza. (Mario Andretti – *World Champion*)

As well as everything else, there was this lizard in the car. I kept trying to reach it to put it out of the car, but it kept getting away from me. It was still there at the end of practice.

Ronnie Peterson on unexpected difficulties during practice at Monza (Mario Andretti – *World Champion*)

PROBLEMS

I don't know why everything keeps going wrong. Somebody at Team Lotus must have run over a nun.

Jochen Rindt

RACING

Racing is 99 per cent boredom and 1 per cent terror.

Geoff Brabham

You win some, lose some, wreck some.

Dale Earnhardt, American driver

The cars came scudding in towards Dublin, running evenly like pellets in the groove of the Naas Road. At the crest of the hill at Inchicore sightseers had gathered in clumps to watch the cars careering homeward and through this channel of poverty and inaction the Continent sped its wealth and industry. Now and again the clumps of people raised the cheer of the gratefully oppressed. Their sympathy, however, was for the blue cars – the cars of their friends, the French.

James Joyce, 'After the Race' (from *Dubliners*)

To me driving is an art form. A painter uses a brush to create something beautiful, my brush is my car. I like my driving to be graceful, beautiful to watch.

John Watson

It is very hard to keep motor racing for many years. But it is also very hard to decide when to stop.

Emerson Fittipaldi

Ninety-five per cent of it is disappointment. But that other 5 per cent outweighs the rest a thousand times over.

Derek Warwick

Motor racing as any racing driver can tell you is a relatively safe sport. It is a clean sport. It is a sporting sport. It is a sport with a real purpose behind it. It is a way of life. It is a homebreaker. It is a disease.

Marshall Pugh, journalist

I race for the money, after all. I try to get top dollar in this business. Still I'd race for nothing. But I wouldn't say that to Colin [Chapman].

Mario Andretti

It is the thrill of danger that gives a surge of adrenalin like I've never known. The fear of death is sensational and unlike anything I have ever done on stage – even the last Wembley concert in front of 80,000 people.

Andrew Ridgeley, the former Wham! star, who had a brief career as a racing driver

When you are out on the circuit you could be racing against your mother and desperate to beat her. All racing drivers want to come first no matter how friendly they may be otherwise.

Damon Hill

In the old days it was much more a Boy's Own, romantic world. If I were to get pretty drunk the night before a race, like drivers in the '50s, I'd be out. I'm a hired hand who arrives at the circuit for practice and leaves straight after the race. I'd like to win the world championship, and I think I will, but I've been racing long enough to know it's 85 per cent disappointment, 10 per cent indifference and 5 per cent elation. The motivation comes from being optimistic about the 5 per cent. You strive for the perfect lap, and in a funny sort of way the actual race is the most peaceful time of a Grand Prix weekend. When you finally get to the grid, there's nothing more you can do. All you have to do is drive as hard and as carefully as you can for an hour and 45 minutes. Then you go home.

Jonathan Palmer

Driving a car is like painting a picture. Anyone can doodle with a pencil. There are plenty of people who can turn out a reasonably recognisable sketch. But the real artists are few and far between. They are born, not made. Driving a car is just as much an art, it is not a knack that can be acquired. Either you have it or you have not.

Mike Hawthorn

It's almost as if you were a painter, your car the brush, the track the canvas. You go out and paint your pictures on the tracks of the world in the way your character dictates. And it is through these pictures that you reveal yourself to the public for what you really are.

Graham Hill

It's like balancing an egg on a spoon while shooting the rapids.

Graham Hill (*The Guinness Dictionary of Sports Quotations*)

RACING

I just like driving a car. When you're on the track, you're on your own. You don't have to speak to anyone.

Nigel Mansell

The cockpit of a racing car is one of the most relaxing places in the world. Early this year, when there were no races for three or four weeks, I mentioned to Maria-Helena that I was feeling something empty in myself. I was missing the racing atmosphere and the racing people.

Emerson Fittipaldi

Motor racing makes me come alive. But it also scares me to death.

James Hunt

To race is to live. But those who died while racing knew, perhaps, how to live more than all others.

Juan Fangio, *Fangio*

A racing career is not only a question of courage and audacity, as so many people think. It is also based on style, leaving nothing to the imagination and all to technique.

Juan Fangio (ibid.)

The more you do, the more you want. The more you need, the more you find out about yourself and the more you understand. There is no end to the knowledge you can get or the peace by going deeper and deeper.

Ayrton Senna

It's not that I like to flirt with danger. To me racing is something of an art – like a painter with oils or a violinist with a bow. I don't get a kick out of speed for speed's sake. I like the challenge – that is of making a 50 mile curve at 51 miles an hour or an 80 mile curve at 85.

Stirling Moss

I race because when the race is finished, the sky is bluer, the women are prettier and the steaks taste better.

Anonymous IndyCar driver (Rich Taylor *Indy: Seventy-Five Years of Racing's Greatest Spectacle*)

Every time I get in a race car, it gets my blood going. The speed, the horsepower, the control. Do it all perfectly, without any mistakes, and that's the best day a man can have.

Al Unser Jr (ibid.)

Do I drive dirty? No, I don't think so – but I can! For me, racing is like a rugby tackle; you've got to go in hard. It has to be clean and fast and positive. When you stick your nose in somewhere half-heartedly – that's when you have a shunt. You have to be ruthless.

Martin Brundle

My overdraft is worth a second a lap to me.

Innes Ireland

Formula One driving is not something you happen to do because you are good at it, or because you enjoy it, or because you once enjoyed it and cannot think of anything better to do. You have to be desperate to drive. You have to force other considerations from your mind.

Nigel Mansell

Motor racing, at almost any level, takes the competitive urge to a further extreme than other sports. It might not dismantle a player's psyche in public in the naked and protracted way that a tennis match can do; it might not take him as far beyond his physical limits as a mountain stage of the Tour de France; it might not require the mad courage of downhill skiing; barring accidents, it will certainly not hurt as much as a boxing match. More than any of these, though, motor racing – head to head and in hot blood – presents a test of manhood.

   Richard Williams, journalist

Motor racing may be a brazen product of the 20th century; but it is strangely gallant. In spirit it is probably nearer the ancient tournaments of knights than any other sport.

   Profile in *The Observer*

I suppose I was fairly successful, but I honestly didn't enjoy it very much. I didn't like the people. I didn't like the bullshit and ballyhoo. I didn't like the parasites who hang around the sport. In a word, it's all crap. They take themselves far too seriously. Motorcycle racers are a nicer bunch of guys altogether. It's a much more down-to-earth type of sport, and it doesn't depend to quite such a degree on the vehicle. I mean, if you don't have a fast enough car, you have no chance. With motorbikes, there's always a little something you can do to push it along.

   Mike Hailwood

Racing is a sickness with us. I couldn't start to explain it, but if you can do it, you do it.

   Mike Hailwood

When I'm in that car, in my own little world, there's no place better.

Nigel Mansell

I didn't just drift into cars because I'm daft about driving. In fact I'm not particularly interested in cars. I wanted to *prove* something to myself. That I could do something well, apart from running the estate.

Sir John Whitmore

Auto-racing is genderless, the car doesn't know the difference and no one can even see that it's a woman driving. No one judges me by my smile or personality, but by my results.

Lyn St James, IndyCar driver

I feel good about my performance, pleased that I was safe and fast and all the things that are not normally associated with first-time races. In fact, I feel like I could cry.

David Coulthard, after his first Grand Prix race

I enjoy it immensely. There is nothing else I have ever enjoyed so much. The pleasure of driving a racing car is something I haven't been able to experience doing anything else. Being able to drive that car and feel the road and be able to take it to its absolute limit – right to the edge . . . I suppose, because it's dangerous, this gives the extra thrill. This is where money doesn't exist.

Jackie Stewart

RACING

Racing isn't all about birds in hot pants and jets flying in and out of circuits. It is about travelling vast distances to spend 10 hours strapped in the car during testing. It's about denying a beer when you want one. It's not all parties. It's about going to bed at 10 p.m. I don't want to sound a martyr, but nothing is for nothing.

Alan Jones

I suppose it's the sense of endeavour that attracts me – and the competition. Motor racing is without the usual apathy that pervades other aspects of life these days.

Colin Chapman

If you believe it can happen to you, how can you possibly do the job properly? If you're never over eight-tenths or whatever, because you're thinking about a shunt, you're not going as quick as you can. And if you're not doing that, you're not a racing driver.

Gilles Villeneuve

By six o'clock on Sunday evening, the race is dead and buried. It doesn't matter whether I won it or lost. I just forget it. If I let myself get eaten up inside by thinking about it, I would have retired years ago.

Nelson Piquet (Mike Doodson, *Nelson Piquet*)

I carry on because motor racing is a disease. You can be distraught with sadness and sorrow because of the people you have lost, when suddenly you have a mental injection and you get into your racing car. At that time you are totally anaesthetised. The past doesn't exist. There are no memories – just driving.

Jackie Stewart

I am able to get to a level where I am ahead of myself; maybe a fifth of a second, who knows? When my car goes into a corner, I am already at the apex.

Ayrton Senna

The day after a race I feel as though I have been trapped in a cement mixer – and then put through a mangle.

Nigel Mansell

All that really counts is the next race.

Niki Lauda

Motor racing is at the same time a sport and a business, it's quite unique. The business bit is easy. You just start off each season and say three million quid for engines, a million for staff, and so on, but professional sport is a very tough way to make a living. There are so many good people out there.

Eddie Jordan

Racing is fun. I enjoy it. If you don't enjoy it, you won't last long.

Al Unser (Rich Taylor, *Indy: Seventy-Five Years of Racing's Greatest Spectacle*)

When the lights go green, he goes red.

Frank Williams, on Nigel Mansell

The straight is only a road connecting the corners and it is on the corners that you try to get ahead.

Stirling Moss

The poetry of a car going round a corner is purely a question of balance. Braking can unbalance a car, just as hard acceleration can, for you are throwing perhaps fifty gallons of juice around. You need a fair amount of guts, but too much is a bad thing. Once a chap goes too fast he's slower, for the moment he loses control he goes sideways.

Stirling Moss

Speed is in your blood. It just won't go away. I couldn't live without it.

Ted Toleman

It is an exercise in calculating risk versus reward. If I reckon I have only a 10 per cent chance of going past an opponent safely, I won't take the chance. The odds have got to be a lot more attractive.

Eddie Irvine

Of course one is aware of the dangers and the medium is a master not to be fooled about with.

John Watson

I do not know whether in Collins' place I would have done the same. It was admirable. A rare gesture of sportsmanship.

Juan Fangio, on Peter Collins, who gave his car to his Argentinian team-mate and nearest rival for the world championship when Fangio's car developed steering problems at Monza in 1956

Once I was in third position when I suddenly saw a car ablaze on the edge of the track. My first thought was; one less, now I'm second.

Enzo Ferrari

I suppose I expend 70 per cent of my energies at the circuit on serving the sponsor. I will admit that usually it's a relief to get out of the hassle and into the car for the race. Then it's just me and the car, alone at last.

Guy Edwards

We did it for Britain and for the hell of it.

Richard Noble, after breaking the world land speed record

In some ways it is a boring track, but there is a certain crazy thrill to hurtling along at over 200 mph on a narrow track between rows of trees. It is like riding a bullet. (*see opposite*)

Damon Hill, on the Hockenheim circuit

Racing is excitement and it is, by definition, dangerous.

Ayrton Senna

The object of the exercise is to finish. That is the only real achievement – to start something difficult and carry it through with the best of your ability, regardless of what happens.

Pat Moss

The fact that you weren't *playing* – that gave it validity.

Stirling Moss

It is my expression of art to drive a car perfectly on a circuit; to be in complete control.

Jochen Rindt

I had tears in my eyes as I crossed the line. It makes nine years' hard work all worthwhile for me.

Mark Blundell, after his third place in the 1993 South Africa Grand Prix

It's a great tribute to my father and to Ayrton that it has taken so long and required someone of such calibre for this record to be broken.

Damon Hill, on Ayrton Senna, who broke Graham Hill's long-standing record of five wins at the Monaco Grand Prix

To improve, and get better, is what I love – and motor racing gives this to me.

Ayrton Senna

It is a totally unreal moment, like a dream, like entering another world. Your spirit goes and the body sets itself free.

Ayrton Senna's description of the start of a race

I don't enjoy racing, it's too bloody dangerous. I enjoy the profits.

James Hunt

A lot of motor racing drivers are not as good at it as they think they are because there are different skills involved. They are used to powering themselves out of trouble, but little mistakes are heavily penalised in a kart, which has more grip than grunt.

Jonathan Tait, marketing manager of Playscape Racing, on karting

Each time I sit in the car I pray to God and Maria to keep me quiet and under control. This helps to keep me technical rather than emotional. It makes me think more and make less mistakes.

Ayrton Senna

On the straight you have a chance to relax your muscles. You can hold the wheel with your knees and wipe the sweat from your brow. It's a moment to compose your thoughts, conserve your energies.

Derek Bell, on racing down the 230 mph Mulsanne straight at Le Mans

If I was suddenly handed a Reliant Robin I would still drive my socks off and get the best out of it that was humanly possible. There's always a chance of winning no matter how badly your car is performing.

Nigel Mansell

It should be about two drivers pitting their skills against each other, not sitting there on the grid worrying about which of the computer programmers programmed their traction control that morning.

David Peevers, publisher of *IndyCar 1993*

It's just as well we're in a closed car. In an open car, they used to bang you on the head as you went by.

Stirling Moss, taking part in the 1987 Mille Miglia

Leading a grand prix is like being prime minister for an hour – you are very conscious of all that depends on your decisions; the millions of pounds invested, the scale of the hopes of the team, the sponsors, and the racing fans – all perhaps decided on your split-second decision on a bend at 200 mph.

Brian James, journalist

The first lap of a stock-car race is horrendous, a wildly horrendous spectacle such as no other sport approaches. Twenty, thirty, forty automobiles, each of them weighing almost two tons, 3700 pounds, with 427-cubic-inch engines, 600 horsepower, are practically together, side by side and tail to nose, on a narrow band of asphalt at 130, 160, 180 miles an hour, hitting the curves so hard the rubber burns off the tyres in front of your eyes.

Tom Wolfe

As soon as I got into that car I thought it the most fun in the world.

Divina Galica

My biggest fear is getting in the way of the big boys and holding up the Niki Laudas. I've had some very good mirrors put in my car and I'll be using them.

Divina Galica

Racing in the rain is so boring, it's not racing at all, it's trying to exist.

Divina Galica

Motor racing is an art, although not recognised as such by the followers of ballet, music and so on. Nevertheless, to me, to watch Fangio drifting round a corner is as exhilarating as seeing a Pavlova executing a graceful pirouette. Being an art one can never finish learning. It may be possible to reach the maximum speed round a given corner in a given car, but there are thousands of corners and many cars, as well as varying surfaces and conditions. This impossibility of reaching perfection gives one much scope for improvement. I always feel that motor racing is rather like chasing the rainbow's end, for the more one learns or the nearer one gets to the end, the further it draws away. It is this ever-disappearing goal which one strives for that makes it the most fascinating of all sports.

Stirling Moss

I am always a bit nervous when I know he is racing. If he is racing at 4.30 I listen to the news. If I haven't heard something by about 5.0 it's all right.

Margaret Thatcher, on her son Mark

I just fear that if I were there he would take that slight risk he would not otherwise take and something might happen.

Margaret Thatcher, explaining why she did not go to watch her son Mark race

I have always preferred to race around circuits, you know what's around the bend. It is fairly reasonable to say that in future my sport will be on circuits rather than the rough bits.

Mark Thatcher, who was rescued after being lost in the Sahara desert while taking part in the Paris to Dakar rally

Nothing should be done in a hurry in racing, except the drive itself; for everything else you need calm.

Alan Jones, *Alan Jones – Driving Ambition*

I had one big fault. I drove always with consideration for the car, whereas to be successful, one must on occasion be prepared to ill-treat it.

Enzo Ferrari (Gerald Donaldson, *Gilles Villeneuve*)

The point is to charge all the time, unless you are first. That's the whole point of racing.

Gilles Villeneuve (ibid.)

Somehow I soon came to feel quite at home in the cockpit of a racing car on 'sticky-wicky' roads. It gave me a sense of security, sitting there snugly behind the tiny windscreen, with all the controls at my fingertips. At times I imagined myself as captain of a submarine, peeping through the periscope, waiting to give orders to my crew; but thank goodness they were not sailors; instead they were just my own hands and feet. So if I were to make a mistake it would cost no other life than my own.

Prince Bira, on driving in the wet (Prince Bira, *Bits and Pieces*)

There is a fundamental point of liberty. If people want to participate in a dangerous sport, they should be free to do so. I wanted to do it, and I knew what the risks were. If someone had told me I had no right to do it, dangerous though it was, I would have bitterly resented it. In my first Formula Two race, on April 7, 1968, Jim Clark was killed. And of the 21 people on the grid that day, four had died by the end of July. I knew what the fatality rate was, but I wanted to do it. And I did it for no money – I paid to do it. If you start prohibiting dangerous sports, you have to prohibit everything – rugby, hang-gliding, mountaineering – never mind the really dangerous things like climbing K2, where you've got a 50 per cent death rate at the moment.

Max Mosley, defending the morality of motor racing following the deaths of Roland Ratzenberger and Ayrton Senna

Sometimes I lost my head. I was finding the limit of the car by exceeding it.

Ukyo Katayama

If you feel clean, tidy and neat, you'll drive cleanly, tidily, neatly and smoothly. If you need a shave, your hair is all over the place and you've got dirty fingernails, I believe you'll have a messy race.

Alan Jones, *Alan Jones – Driving Ambition*

There's no question that motor racing is a very sexual sport. There's no doubt about it. I must say that after a long race I feel particularly sexy.

Graham Hill (Andrew Malkovich, *Sports Quotations*)

When you're driving hard out on the limit and the true love of speed comes over you, you don't want to slow up. It's always the same: the faster you go, the less you care about being able to stop – ever.

Sam Posey, American driver (ibid.)

My biggest concern during a race is being bored. The biggest thing I have to combat is falling asleep while going round and round. All drivers have little games they play to keep alert. I try to pick out landmarks – sometimes people in the crowd – and look at them every time around. I've startled more than a few of my friends by waving as I go through a turn.

Mario Andretti (ibid.)

Speed? Really the whole process is the reverse of speed, how to eliminate it. It doesn't exist for me except when I am driving poorly. Then things seem to be coming at me quickly instead of passing in slow motion and I know I'm off form.

Jackie Stewart (Frank Keating, *Caught by Keating*)

Kart racing is a tumultous experience and they dart round a track like a shoal of nervous fish.

Christopher Hilton, *Alain Prost*

It is a profession in which one is always an apprentice.

Keke Rosberg (Keke Rosberg and Keith Botsford, *Keke – An Autobiography*)

During the run there is a panorama of feeling and sensation. Gorgeous colours, a feeling of weightlessness, a sense of everything being quiet, an overwhelming sense of accomplishment. Yeah, it's freaky as hell.

Jack Maclure, drag racer (Jonathon Green and Don Atyeo, *The Book of Sports Quotes*)

Cornering is like bringing a woman to a climax. Both you and the car must work together. You start to enter the area of excitement at the corner, you set up a pace which is right for the car and after you've told it it is coming along with you, you guide it along at a rhythm which by now has become natural. Only after you've cleared the corner can you both take pleasure in knowing that it's gone well.

Jackie Stewart (ibid.)

I've never seen driving as a sexual thing – I just could never consider it in that light. I think women are interested in the drivers because of the dangers, but some of us are as dull as Old Nick.

Jackie Stewart (ibid.)

Mom's chilli was worth an extra two miles per hour.

Bobby Unser (ibid.)

This rally is good for us. If you haven't reached Timbuktu, you haven't really succeeded in the race.

Alassane Dicko, secretary-general of the Timbuktu town hall, on the Paris–Dakar rally

It's a violent sport, and not just because of the danger, but because of the power of the machinery involved. I get satisfaction out of taming that power and making it look unviolent.

John Watson (Andrew Longmore, *Moments of Greatness, Touches of Class*)

It's like trying to describe the taste of an orange, it's so difficult to put into words. It's a race of changing moods. Everything is crisp and bright and shining new when you start – and off you go. Then the light fades and the dusk comes on. Driving in the half-light, it's easy to make mistakes. Although there shouldn't be anyone coming towards you, it's easy to overshoot the bends which you can't see properly. As you pass the end of the pits the most delicious smell of crêpe suzette wafts across the track, and the night falls.

Alain de Cadenet, on driving in the Le Mans race

It's the excitement and the thrill of beating obstacles that the rules and the weather bring against you. Also the danger it brings. I like the skid one gets on ice and the feel of being master in spite of it.

Nancy Mitchell, rally driver in the 1950s

Racing makes me steady.

Prince Bira of Siam

I'm only 25 years old and have plenty of time to win the championship on my own.

Peter Collins, explaining why he gave his car to Fangio, who was forced to retire his car during the 1956 Italian Grand Prix (Brock Yates, *Enzo Ferrari*)

It's an outlet for people whose lives and selves are inadequate. They try to put order and meaning into their lives by imposing their will on something potentially chaotic. A racer believes he can make his deadly machine safe. He plays God. He is one of the Blessed. His sport *must* be deadly so that in competing and surviving his skill takes on mystical qualities.

Phil Hill (Phil Berger and Larry Bortstein, *The Boys of Indy*)

And that's what it's about. Trying to get the car to feel like part of your body. An extension. I get my mind into part of the machinery. And get it to be . . . like the tyres are made of rubber, sure. But when things are right, you can feel the tyres in your nerve ends. And when you take a car down into the corner as deep as it'll go and you know it's on the ragged edge, it's just like a shot in the arm. It's such a gratifying feeling that you've taken a piece of machinery and kind of glued yourself to it.

Johnny Parsons, IndyCar driver (ibid.)

The service is not over until after the benediction.

Bernd Rosemeyer (Elly Rosemeyer and Chris Nixon, *Rosemeyer*)

In motor racing, as in so many other fields of civilised human activity, Italy provides the essence of romance.

Mike Lawrence, writer (*The Mille Miglia*)

Like my father, like all those who embrace this career, I only obey my instinct: without it, I would not know how to live, I would not succeed in making any sense of my days.

Alberto Ascari (Kevin Desmond, *The Man with Two Shadows*)

I have often been asked, 'What is the good of motor racing?' The shortest answer that I can give is that in common with all other forms of competition, it plays a part in developing the breed. The motor car of today and its accessories, whether a public service or a private vehicle, would never have reached the pitch of development which it has, had it not been for the supreme test to which it has been put, and the important lessons thereby learned in motor racing.

Sir Tim Birkin, *Full Throttle*

Pole can be decided by thousandths of a second, an Einstein (well, Einsteinian) concept of time as hard to comprehend as his Theory of Relativity.

Christopher Hilton, *Gerhard Berger: The Human Face of Formula One*

The meltdown to the Italian Grand Prix is high voltage and that's not just because of the weight of so much history bearing down on the present, never mind offering tributes to the memory of Enzo Ferrari. You cannot avoid knowing that this is an important place graced by virtually every great driver. The high voltage is the howl of the *tifosi* which grunts to a grumble to a yearn to a wild, wild shriek before the cars get a chance to shriek themselves. It's a mighty backdrop of banners and flags and home-made slogans full round the teeming circuit. The grid, arranged on such a broad, imperial sweep of a straight, seems more than usually important as if spread on a great canvas. The arrival of the cars on the dummy grid, long long minutes before the parade lap, becomes an event, the earthy thousands in the grandstands hissing some, applauding others and detonating when the Ferraris appear. It is at this moment, if he hasn't done it before, that the Ferrari driver must isolate the emotion or perish with it.

Christopher Hilton (ibid.)

They have the most astounding audacity in some parts of Europe. For instance, there is going to be a Grand Prix at Monaco – a Grand Prix, mark you, in a Principality which does not possess a single open road of any length, but has only ledges on the face of a cliff and the ordinary main thoroughfares that everyone who has been to the Casino knows so well.

Autocar (1928)

I like the competition better than the victory, the fighting better than the winning.

Stirling Moss (Robert Daley, *The Cruel Sport*)

If you took all the danger out of racing I'd enjoy it three times more, a hundred times more.

Jo Bonnier (Peter Manso, *Vroom*)

There's no perfect race. It's a fact, so it doesn't do any good to stew over it.

Dan Gurney (ibid.)

Grand Prix racing is a calculated risk accepted by those who take part in it. No regulations could be drawn up which would guarantee safety. If you take away the normal hazards of motor racing you take away the reasons for going motor racing – and this applies to any venture into the comparative unknown.

Mike Hawthorn, *Champion Year*

This race is stupid – it achieves nothing. I'll never take part in it again as long as it is such a Derby Day affair.

Stirling Moss on the Le Mans race

The car was so good it was just a question of taking her round like a taxi driver in the final stint.

Derek Warwick, after winning the 1992 Le Mans race

Grand Prix racing is more money, more speed, more skill, more tension, more danger, more triumph, more tragedy. Grand Prix racing is the ultimate. Grand Prix racing is the Himalayas; all else is the Catskills.

Robert Daley, *The Cruel Sport*

Rather as good coffee houses grind freshly roasted beans and waft the aroma towards passers by, so does drag racing commend itself to the neighbourhood by the shattering noise of high revs and the intense smell of enriched fuel.

Sir Clement Freud, journalist and wit

A lot of drivers try to make it sound like a more spiritual thing. But the basic truth is you get a great big buzz out of driving a racing car very quickly.

Damon Hill

RETIREMENT

The black cloud has gone. I lived with it for nearly 11 years. It was there day and night. It was there between races and it was even there between racing seasons. Ironically, the only time it ever disappeared was when you actually got into the car and drove.

James Hunt

It is time to grow up. Now I will start some sensible work.

Niki Lauda, announcing his retirement for the second time

My 'family' has gone. In ten years 20 of my best friends died behind the wheel. I am 47. I am tired in body and spirit. I don't want to finish up like my friends.

Juan Fangio

Champions, actors and dictators should always retire when they are at the top.

Juan Fangio

If I'd been a tennis player I'd have done one more year just for the money – but motor racing is not like that. You can't go out there with all the dangers and do the job just for the money.

Jody Scheckter

RETIREMENT

I look back on my career as one of absolute pleasure along with a guilty feeling of selfishness in being separated from my family. They have supported me throughout my racing years, and the time has now come for me to throw off the increasing demands of a Grand Prix driver and spend more time with my family and with my business interests.

Sir Jack Brabham

There I was going round the track at God knows what speed when I suddenly thought, 'Why am I doing this? It's daft. There are other things in life than this.'

Niki Lauda, explaining his retirement from racing during the Canadian Grand Prix in 1979

If Australia could be 50 miles off the coast of England then I'd probably go on. The trouble is every time I go away, I miss my farm.

Alan Jones, announcing his retirement

People who do something special, like Grand Prix racing, have the right to stop whenever they like. Because they risk their lives. I know people didn't like the way I did it, but that was the only way I could do it. I maintained my own freedom. It proves the sport is not controlled by television, or sponsors, or managers, but that the people who have to drive are human beings and should be able to decide their own lives. If people don't like what I did, they should get in a car and try it themselves.

Niki Lauda

Last week my son said it was about time I should retire. I asked him what I should do instead and he replied, 'Write some books and drive the school bus.'

Jackie Stewart

I first went to a race when I was 16 and thought, that's me. Twenty years later, I was going round Brands Hatch. I thought, this is hard work. When the passion goes, you must go.

Guy Edwards

The truth is I cannot afford to die – because of death duties. I have a million pounds' worth of headaches.

Sir John Whitmore, explaining his retirement

I hate to get emotional like this, but for 35 years I've been looking up there, looking at the people, trying to produce for them. It's a hard decision but there comes a time.

A. J. Foyt, announcing his retirement

It's like a nightmare, to be honest, like a nightmare.

A. J. Foyt, after retirement

I have felt tremendous guilt at doing something that I know is absolutely selfish and now, financially, has been unnecessary. Modern society does not really allow this extremity of living. Maybe bull-fighting has it. Maybe mountaineering comes near it. I don't really know.

Jackie Stewart, announcing his retirement

Drivers like Jackie Stewart were intelligent enough to make a complete break when they retired, but I couldn't resist sneaking back. Although nothing like as fast as I used to be, I'm still a racer at heart.

Stirling Moss

RETIREMENT

One day when I retire, my ambition is to go back to being a normal person – one who likes other people, whom other people like.

James Hunt

It's very tempting and I'm very flattered but money isn't everything and this offer does not change the reasons I retired. Safety for Grand Prix drivers was the main one and until it has been made patently more safe for drivers, I have no intention of even thinking of unretiring.

James Hunt, turning down a lucrative offer from Marlboro-McLaren to come out of retirement

I came to the conclusion while driving that it would be foolish to continue, because I have lost a certain amount of dexterity.

Stirling Moss

One must retire some time, while the going is good. Once a year I have a board meeting with myself, asking whether I am as quick as I was, what the opposition is.

Roy Salvadori

When do you give up racing? When do you give up making love?

Stirling Moss

When you have given 100 per cent and you know what that is like, then you know when you can't give 100 per cent.

Al Unser Sr

When do you give up racing? When do you give up making love?

Stirling Moss

With racing in general and F1 in particular there is a
considerable risk of an accident. I've taken that chance
throughout my career and, after four world titles without
a serious accident, I don't want to tempt the devil for ever.

Alain Prost

The thought of quitting grows on a driver little by little. He
finds himself thinking about it more and more. It seems ever
more desirable. He sleeps a little less after each race. He
enjoys driving a little less. His edge goes off, his appetite
diminishes. Courage comes when a driver recognises that
moment and quits.

Alan Jones, *Alan Jones – Driving Ambition*

All my life I've always had the next race to look forward to.
Even when I've had bad days, I could always say 'I've got
another chance next week, or at this track next year.' Now
I can't say that any more.

Mario Andretti

SAFETY

The thing that terrifies me most is taking my car out to the M25. There really are some nutters out on the roads these days.

Johnny Herbert

I take all the safety measures I can but once on the track I don't give it a moment's thought. Worrying about dying won't make it any safer, but it will make it slower.

Jonathan Palmer

Much of the motoring press and many of the older generation of racing drivers were convinced I was anaesthetising some holy ritual. They seemed to think that drivers were paid for risking their lives, not exercising their skill.

Jackie Stewart, defending himself against criticism that he was too safety-conscious

If you travel at the speeds we are driving at accidents will happen whether they come from driver errors, mechanical errors or acts of God. I want to take out the unnecessary risks, the telegraph poles beside a track, unguarded trees and the sections where a car could easily crash into spectators.

Jackie Stewart

The truth of the matter is that, generally speaking, drivers are interested in having the fastest car. They are not really interested in safety – that is our responsibility and something to which we give constant thought and attention. If you said to a racing driver 'Here are two cars, one is very dangerous and one is very safe but the dangerous one is five seconds a lap quicker than the safe one' they will all – and they would admit it without exception – go into the dangerous one.

Max Mosley

Brakes only slow you up.

Tazio Nuvolari

One of the interesting aspects of my presence at the races is that the drivers who know me like to see the father-figure arriving and to know that I'm around. That, I think, has helped a lot, because in the circumstances of a big accident it is sometimes hard for a driver to know who is actually trying to help him.

Prof. Sidney Watkins, head of the medical panel for the International Motor Sports Federation

Personally I don't feel it necessary for me to prove my bravery by driving in shirt sleeves on a circuit which is unnecessarily dangerous to myself, the other drivers, spectators or racing fraternity. This is more a sign of irresponsibility than anything else. With the help of the experts I equip myself with what I consider to be the finest and safest racing attire available; I also expect, and in fact demand, from my entrant or constructor this high standard in my racing cars.

Jackie Stewart

We are all looking for a way in which we don't have to cut trees down. But, if necessary, then we have to face the situation. What is more important, the life of a human being or a tree?

Michael Schumacher, on the possibility of having to cut down trees in order to make Monza safer

I think the drivers today are guilty of being lazy, apathetic and lethargic. The drivers are the ultimate experts and they must fight to have a proper say concerning safety. It is difficult. There are a lot of people among the organisers, governing bodies and track designers who are selfishly protecting their own little domain, but the driver's view must prevail.

Jackie Stewart

There's no logic or plan to life. There are no rules to say if you play safe, you will go on to be 100 and happy.

Damon Hill

You can't wrap yourself in cotton wool. I have had a lot of lucky escapes, but sod it, it's my office. I go to work in a Grand Prix car and I love it.

Martin Brundle

Safety and money you should not mix up.

Gerhard Berger

[Jackie] Stewart was the one who started all this crap, going about with his blood group on his underpants and things.

Innes Ireland (Peter Manso, *Vroom*)

SAFETY

I must stress that I do not wish to see anything like the death rate of the fifties. But I think you cannot totally eliminate risk from grand prix racing and that is what they seem to be trying to do. And then some of the drivers ask for £1 million per race. Words fail me . . .

Tony Brooks

SAYINGS

When the flag drops, the bullshit stops.

Anon

BRM – Blooming Rotten Motors

Anon

The right crowd and no crowding.

Advertising slogan for Brooklands

Win on Sunday, sell on Monday.

Saying in the US car industry, possibly by Lee Iacocca (Rich Taylor, *Indy: Seventy-Five Years of Racing's Greatest Spectacle*)

If you can race, you can *race*.

Anon

To finish first you must first finish.

Anon

Gentlemen and Lady, start your engines please.

The starter's instruction to drivers at the Indianapolis 500

SAYINGS

We Are Still Royalists Because Nigel Is Still King Of The Poms

Banner supporting Nigel Mansell at the Australian IndyCar Grand Prix

Nigel – Our Real Royal Family On Tour

ibid.

Finger trouble

Euphemism for human error

A Mars a Day Helps You Work, Rest and Play.

Slogan created by Murray Walker

Rooting you out of the groove.

An American phrase to describe what the pursuing driver is attempting to do to the driver in front

There's a saying in racing that you think you're holding the wheel, but then you find out it's holding you.

Mark Donohue (Phil Berger and Larry Bortstein, *The Boys of Indy*)

Eat, Drink and be Merry.

Innes Ireland's approach to life (Innes Ireland, *All Arms and Elbows*)

Pedal to the metal.

Going flat out

SELF-IMAGE

I never considered a car as an instrument to achieve an end, but as part of myself, or better, I was part of the car, like a piston or gear.

Juan Fangio

I was always a devil and that is the truth.

Tazio Nuvolari

The trouble is that I'm a domineering character – and yet I want to be dominated.

Rosemary Smith, Irish rally driver in the '60s and '70s

All my life I have been lucky.

Juan Fangio

To the spectators I am a crash helmet buried inside a car that is flashing past at 200 mph. I'm a fleeting glimpse of humanity. I've had more recognition from two appearances on *Question of Sport* than anything I've done in F1.

Martin Brundle

I'm a racer and a purist. I think Formula One is too technical now.

Nigel Mansell

Although I do not have the gift of the gab and am completely charmless, I just persevere. I never give up.

Damon Hill

I don't like people calling me the Earl of Dumfries and all that rubbish. I don't want anyone to think I am some sort of aristocrat just dabbling in motor racing for fun.

Johnny Dumfries, then the Earl of Dumfries, now the Marquess of Bute

I have a certain peasant cunning. A bit of good old common sense.

Niki Lauda, *To Hell and Back*

I never forget. I never ever, ever forget, ever.

Ron Dennis (Christopher Hilton, *Gerhard Berger: The Human Face of Formula One*)

I'm in the wrong business. I don't want to beat anybody. I don't want to be a big hero. I'm a peace-loving man, basically.

Phil Hill (Robert Daley, *The Cruel Sport*)

I'm not a particularly good team man. I don't see myself as sitting quietly in the background helping the team along. I feel as if the team should be helping me.

Jackie Stewart (Peter Manso, *Vroom*)

I sometimes think I'm a little bit more English than French.

Alain Prost

115

No one has to second-guess where they are with me. I say it as it is. I walk a straight line in life. I don't have a character that I switch on and switch off. I'm not good at politics. I don't want to be. I'm not good at being evasive.

Nigel Mansell

I've got to keep trying something new and I've got to win at it. I've been a ferocious competitor from the moment I could think.

James Hunt

I am a racing driver – it is what I do. I don't dwell on the dangers but I recognise them.

Lyn St James, IndyCar driver

I am inclined to go over the top and I know it. I am communicating an electric situation.

Murray Walker

I'm deeply insecure, like most sportsmen, and I have to prove myself over and over to people who have doubted me.

Damon Hill

I've never considered myself a particularly brave person, nor, really, do I want to. My racing certainly isn't brave, not in the sense, say, of bullfighting.

Jackie Stewart (Jackie Stewart and Peter Manso, *Faster*)

I dearly love having a go. Nothing pleases me more. Psychologically, I don't like being on pole. Inside me, I think I prefer being on the second row so I can work someone over.

Alan Jones, *Alan Jones – Driving Ambition*

An agitator of men.

Enzo Ferrari (Brock Yates, *Enzo Ferrari*)

I don't like being known as an engineer . . . I'm someone who sits around and thinks. Sometimes I think about motorcar engines.

Keith Duckworth

I was a physical leader. I learned to become a mental leader.

Frank Williams

On some occasions, I should probably have been a bit more selfish. In a racing driver, not to be seems to be considered a weakness, but it's not my natural way. Even if I have in my contract priority when it comes to new parts for the car, or whatever, I'll tend to pass it up, for the sake of keeping harmony in the team. In this business, I guess you shouldn't be like that. The great champions don't behave that way.

Gerhard Berger

I am not an escapist, I like reality.

Bernie Ecclestone

My personality is to be committed, to go my own way.

Ayrton Senna

In a world where so many people lead relatively unexciting lives I think I am a privileged person. And because I feel that, I think I alway try to work harder to justify my position of privilege. We have only one life and I think we have a responsibilty to try and make the best of it.

John Watson

I have no nationality. I have forgotten my nationality. I am above nationalities. I am truly a world president. I work as best I can for the general good.

Jean-Marie Balestre, then president of Fisa

I am the boss and you all know what a boss is. A boss is a boss.

Jean-Marie Balestre

I'm not superstitious, nor terribly religious, but I am C of E [Church of England].

Graham Hill

If I was in the armed forces, I'd be working under cover. I'm a more secretive type.

Damon Hill

SHUNTS

It doesn't give me pause for thought, in that I might give up. It makes me angry. I feel sorry for the survivors, the family, but more than anything else, I feel angry at the unfairness of it all. Not angry at the car manufacturers, or the competition organisers, angry at God, maybe. It is a pretty primitive reaction.

Jonathan Palmer

When a driver dies, he goes out doing exactly what he wants to do. I don't find that depressing at all. If I'm going to die, which I probably will, I hope it's doing something I want to do.

Bernie Ecclestone

It was worse than war, if that is possible. There was a terrific explosion and two car wheels whistled over my head. A piece of metal hit me square on the forehead. When I got up a few seconds later I had a queer feeling that I was back to the time when I was a soldier in Alsace and a bomb fell in the middle of my section. It was the same sight – wounded people sitting, lying, standing, screaming with fear. And all the time you could hear the cars still running and the strains of an accordion coming over the loudspeakers.

Jacques Lelong, a spectator at the 1955 Le Mans race when 88 people were killed

I cursed motor racing and all who took part in it, not least myself. Most of all at that moment I hated the cars, those cold, shining, soulless monsters that can consume a man. They are death traps, made to measure like a Savile Row suit.

> Alfred Neubauer, on the death of Richard Seaman during the 1939 Belgian Grand Prix

The accident didn't hurt me at all. It's an honour to have been under your wheels. I was more worried about you. I have followed you all over and now I've met you face to face. It really is a dream come true. (*see opposite*)

> Spectator Ian Neild, who fell under Nigel Mansell's car during chaotic scenes at the end of the 1992 British Grand Prix

I got straight up and said to Nigel, 'I'm all right, can I have your helmet?'

> Ian Neild

All the cars practising had pulled up and with all the drivers bending over me the place looked like a drivers' convention.

> Stirling Moss after his accident while practising for the 1960 Belgian Grand Prix

The only time I've prayed recently was after Gerhard Berger's accident. I just had to thank the Almighty that he was okay. But I don't pray for myself. Oh no, that would be cheating. It wouldn't be fair for me to pursue this career and expect everyone to look after me – least of all God.

> Derek Warwick

Unhappily, motor racing is also this.

> Mario Andretti, reacting to the news of Ronnie Peterson's death
> (Mario Andretti – *World Champion*)

You appreciate that it is very easy to die and you have to arrange your life to cope with that reality.

> Niki Lauda

I don't mind having an accident when I can see it coming.

> Nigel Mansell

At times like this we have to be thankful for all the hard work that people like Jackie Stewart, Niki Lauda, Alain Prost, Ayrton Senna and Fisa have done over the years to improve safety standards.

> Derek Warwick, after his 150 mph crash at the 1990 Italian
> Grand Prix

The Angels of Imola.

> The name given to the marshals who dragged an unconscious Gerhard
> Berger from his blazing car after crashing at Imola in 1989

I can't really describe how bad it's been. I don't want to harp on but I think it's worth talking about. I'm sure there are people who can understand because of things that have happened in their lives, but it's difficult to describe what I was feeling like at Imola that Saturday afternoon. To stand on the pit wall and see a friend of mine, because Roland was a friend, to see him die the way he did with all the attempts to resuscitate him . . . it's making the hairs on the back of my neck stand up now talking about it, all these weeks later. I'm only 28. I haven't had much experience in life, and fortunately I haven't had people in my family or close relations die. Not that anything can prepare you for that, and it comes back in waves. You concentrate on things again and time is a great healer, but you still get these fluctuations and you think about it.

Nick Wirth, boss of Simtek, on the death of his driver Roland Ratzenberger

Try now to mix the image of Senna the man and Senna the myth and add the spectacle which his death became. What you are left with is that monster which the media left us with, a tragedy without boundaries, the most astonishing tragedy on the planet, more penetrating than the blood spilt in Bosnia or Rwanda.

The Italian newspaper *Gazzetta dello Sport* reporting Ayrton Senna's accident

Reasons for joy and pride are few and far between in Brazil. Our country has had to live with the hard reality of political corruption beyond comprehension; of absurd violence, drug dealing and frequent kidnapping, all of which prosper in beautiful cities like Rio de Janeiro. Inflation is now so high across the country that we have had to double our efforts just to maintain the same modest standard of living. But then, on a Sunday morning, Senna would relieve us from this pain. Time and again on an F1 weekend, he would demonstrate to us that winning always comes down to the individual. He taught us the values of commitment, competence and seriousness. He kept our faith in the future alive.

Lito Cavalcanti, journalist

In his honour I will never sit in an F1 car again. He was master of his craft. I was proud to race against him.

Alain Prost, after Ayrton Senna's fatal accident

Suddenly, as if he had been struck by an invisible fist, his car was swept off the track into the woods.

Driver Chris Irwin describing Jim Clark's fatal accident

There are no miracles in life. I stayed alive because I was 100 per cent fit before the accident. I was fit because I wanted to be fit. I stayed alive because I willed myself alive. I recovered so quickly because I wanted to recover so quickly. I worked day and night to recover.

Niki Lauda

Racing drivers are meant to die in furious petrol fires when they have outrun their luck on a corner named after its last wildcat victim. They aren't meant to die of the prosaic, daily, deadly malfunctions that kill the rest of us. They are supposed to die explosively, not according to the predictions of an insurance agent's actuarial tables.

Peter Silverton, journalist

He should have been encouraging me to fight for life, not giving me a helping hand into death.

Niki Lauda, on the priest who gave him the last rites after his crash at the Nurburgring in 1976

Motor racing has always been dangerous, and it takes a weekend like this to scrape away that very thin veneer of apparent safety.

Damon Hill, on the deaths of Roland Ratzenberger and Ayrton Senna

SHUNTS

The poet of speed is dead.

El Diario, Bolivian newspaper, on Ayrton Senna

Motor sport's myopia has never been more clearly seen than in this weekend. Three successive days of practice and racing at the San Marino Grand Prix produced three horrific accidents. Not all of them were fatal, but all of them could have been. As the toll mounted, someone should have called a halt, partly out of respect, partly out of prudence. No one did so. Grand Prix racing failed to react appropriately. Its attitude was to get the bodies off the track and get the race restarted. Those in charge of San Marino seemed more concerned to honour their television and sponsorship contracts than to honour their slain. At the post-race press conference, two of the winning drivers seemed incapable of thinking of anything except the fact that they had finished in the top three. Only the winner Michael Schumacher seemed aware of the seriousness of the questions which must now be asked about a sport which is currently producing unacceptable risks and unacceptable entertainment.

Leading article in *The Guardian*

We were all left feeling totally exposed, vulnerable. We all felt, 'If it can happen to Jimmy, what chance have we got?'

Chris Amon, on the death of Jim Clark in 1968

I don't know what happened, but I think it was quick. I feel okay. It is a bit difficult to breathe because of my nose and my hand hurts a bit. I'm off to play with the nurses now.

Rubens Barrichello, after his accident during qualifying for the San Marino Grand Prix

The show at Imola went on despite everything and death itself was made into a brutal spectacle. The roar of the motors and the spark of the sponsors prevailed over death, silencing man.

The Vatican newspaper *L'Osservatore Romano*, on the 1994 San Marino Grand Prix

Williams will find a replacement driver. Formula One won't.

Tribute placed outside the Williams headquarters at Didcot after Ayrton Senna's fatal accident

There is, behind motor racing, a strange and terrifying brutality. The process of natural selection is carried out with no mercy and without regard to past performances. Whatever evil god governs the sport wields the chopper and, *bang* a driver is gone. More often than not, there is neither rhyme nor reason about it.

Richard Garrett, *The Motor Racing Story*

My consolation is that if I were to have a fatal accident, up to the minute of my death I would have been doing something I wanted to do more than anything else in the world. I would have lived a life on the highest level of personal fulfilment and pleasure.

John Watson

I noticed about 500 metres before the chicane that the left tyre had lost air. Then it just exploded. I just remember my helmet pounding on the asphalt many times.

Ayrton Senna, after crashing during testing at Hockenheim in 1991

I have never been to a motor race before – it was like something from *Mad Max 2*.

A shocked spectator after an accident at Oulton Park

Brazil had two hopes. Now there is one.

Brazilian football coach Carlos Alberto Pareira, on the weight of expectations facing his team in the World Cup after the death of Ayrton Senna

You get depressed of course, when you crash, or when somebody is killed. Maybe some people even give a thought to retiring. But few ever do.

Mike Hailwood

I never thought this would happen to me but perhaps it's a test you have to go through, a way of finding out about yourself. All I know is I still want to race.

Johnny Herbert, after his accident at Brands Hatch in 1988

He had no chance to get out. He went off on the fastest part of the circuit. He went up the bank and into the fence. How many drivers have got to die before they do something? I have been trying to get them to get down the banks and put barriers in their stead. If a life is at stake that is all that matters and they should put the circuits in safety order first.

Jackie Stewart, on the death of Piers Courage at the Dutch Grand Prix in 1970

When I was knocked out in Sweden I came round and was able to diagnose for rescuers that I needed a blood drip immediately.

Jonathan Palmer, a qualified doctor

It has been a very difficult time for me personally and for everyone. When your five-year-old daughter comes and asks you if it is true that Senna is dead, then it is hard to reconcile things.

Martin Brundle

Death and danger are all part of the sport, and we are all willing to take the risks. All I know is that if it happened to me I wouldn't expect anyone to call the race off.

Johnny Herbert, rejecting suggestions that the 1994 Monaco Grand Prix should be called off after Karl Wendlinger's accident during practice

I'll make two or three laps. I'll drive slowly.

Alberto Ascari's last words before his fatal accident

I just rolled with the punch and it didn't hurt a bit.

Boxer Barry McGuigan, after a crash at Silverstone

The brain scan was normal, but I said it was wrong, it has never been normal.

Nigel Mansell, after crashing during practice for the Phoenix IndyCar race

Racing is a terribly horrible gamble. When a driver makes a mistake, he's going at his slowest, round a corner. When a car makes a mistake and gives out, it's going at its fastest, on the straight.

James Hunt

Just find a goddamn hammer and knock me upside of
the head.

A. J. Foyt to rescuers, after morphine had no effect on the pain
following his crash at Riverside, California in 1965

These useless follies must be stopped. Too many people who
have nothing to do with the race lose their lives every year.

The then Bishop of Mantua, following the deaths of 12 people in the
1957 Mille Miglia

One split, one mistake, one separation of a vital component
is all it takes to bring death in the afternoon. For those are
the men who drive with their own ghosts peering back at
them from the rear-view mirror.

Report in *The Sun*

He was a mystical character who periodically portrayed
himself as a martyr. He did not really belong to a sporting
world, populated by mediocrities. His pursuit of truth, of
self-knowledge, was more suited to the seminary than the
racetrack.

The Daily Telegraph, on Ayrton Senna

Ayrton [Senna] seemed bullet-proof.

Nigel Mansell

In the Monaco paddock, it is as if someone has dimmed the
lights and turned down the volume. Familiar faces seem to
have aged. The mechanics go efficiently about their work,
as usual, but their expressions are taut. It has always been
this way when tragedy has been visited upon Formula One,
but after an interval of 12 years, the shock is all the greater
and for many, a new experience.

Nigel Roebuck, journalist

Your son and I were great rivals but in the end it was this which made us so close. I can never forget him because his life became my life, and mine became his. So part of me has gone with Ayrton.

Part of a letter that Nigel Mansell sent to Ayrton Senna's father, Milton da Silva

I took one bend too many too fast. I was an accident waiting to happen.

Frank Williams, on his crash on a country road in France in 1986

My helmet came off on the first roll, and everyone thought it was my head bouncing about.

Julian Bailey, after an accident at Snetterton

This is what I feared would happen. It is disgraceful. The track was just not safe enough. I am very, very, very upset. I still can't think why it should have been allowed to happen. Everyone is a bit at fault – the drivers themselves as well as the organisers but most of all the CSI [International Sporting Commission] because they had the last word and voted the race should go ahead. I decided last night not to take part. My life is more important than money. I am very disappointed with my fellow drivers because we had been pushing hard for security and safety and I cannot understand why the drivers decided to go ahead and race.

Emmerson Fittipaldi, after four people were killed and nine injured at the 1975 Spanish Grand Prix

Everyone who goes motor racing, both drivers and spectators, knows what the situation is and you do not stop a war because people get hurt.

Stirling Moss

For many years, people from all over the world have shared with us their great admiration for our dear Ayrton Senna; someone who believed in working to make dreams come true; someone who always tried to improve in every aspect of his life; someone to whom life was filled with happiness; someone who deeply loved his country. With the green and yellow flag of Brazil in his hands after each victory, Ayrton demonstrated with pride how much he believed in his country, and in his fellow Brazilian citizens who always loved and supported him. We now find comfort in our deepest belief that Ayrton's same ideals will endure throughout the world; ideals of solidarity and faith. God bless our friends from all nations who have demonstrated so much love and sympathy for us at this moment of pain and sorrow. Thank you.

A letter to *Autosport* from Ayrton Senna's family

We are all bloody mercenaries and we can't get hysterical every time someone gets killed. If you wept over each death during a civil war in the Congo, you'd have no business being a mercenary. It wouldn't work in the Congo; it won't work on the circuit.

Alan Jones, *Alan Jones – Driving Ambition*

There are huge, loud noises, there are wrenches and twists, lurches, bangs, forces twisting you every which way; it's like being set upon by a gang of thugs in an alley.

Alan Jones (ibid.)

As for the accidents and tragedy – the circus goes on. There is no room for tears.

François Cevert, the day before he was killed

On the day of the race, a lot of people want you to sign something just before you get in the car so that they can say they got your last autograph.

A. J. Foyt (Andrew Malkovich, *Sports Quotations*)

I'd rather have an accident than fall in love. That's how much I love motor racing.

Lella Lombardi (Frank Keating, *Caught by Keating*)

When the car somersaulted at 280 mph when I was going for the record, my only thought was, 'God, the wife is going to kill me for this.'

Barry Bowles (ibid.)

If I live too long, if I live beyond the next race, or tomorrow, I don't know what I'd do with myself.

Patrick Depailler (Keith Botsford, *The Champions of Formula One*)

When you've brushed with death it's human to wonder if maybe it is your turn coming. Everything in life is sweetened by risk.

Peter Revson (Jonathon Green and Don Atyeo, *The Book of Sports Quotes*)

You just have to treat death like any other part of life.

Tom Sneva, US racing driver (ibid.)

You can't see anything. I couldn't open the seat belts because I was panicking. I was thinking that they'd forgotten me.

Jos Verstappen, after his car was engulfed by fire while refuelling during the 1994 German Grand Prix

The Mille Miglia, Cemetery of Babies and Men. Enough!

A headline in the Italian newspaper *Corriere d'Informazione*

A driver's first reaction when he goes off the track and is unhurt is one of humiliation. If it's just a spin and you haven't tangled with anyone, you make up your mind to be more careful – even though you've lost much ground. Also, all the way back to the pits you will be busy trying to make up a reasonable excuse.

Evelyn Mull, American racer in the 1950s (Evelyn Mull, *Women in Sports Car Competition*)

When I had my accident at Monza in 1952, I woke up in hospital and understood that it was very easy to go from life to death without even knowing it. And I understood something else as well: now that I had been injured, the people who surrounded me began to leave, thinking that my racing days were over. I learned who my true friends were.

Juan Fangio (Juan Fangio with Roberto Carozzo, *My Racing Life*)

It's one thing to go into a corner when you have a wall, or ditch, or trees, and you know that to beat the other guy you have to go in faster than him while at the same time realising a mistake could be fatal. It is a totally different challenge to being able to go into a corner, spin into the gravel and say, 'Oops, I've overdone it. What a shame!' That's not grand prix racing.

Tony Brooks

SPARES

Someone said I was involved in the Great Train Robbery. Incredible really. Why would I want to rob a train with only £1 million on it? That's not even enough to pay one driver. I suppose it doesn't hurt to have people thinking things like that.

Bernie Ecclestone

I've been wheeling and dealing since I was 11, buying and selling fountain pens, bicycles, what have you. Then I went into motor-cycles, cars, property – whatever was about. I suppose entrepreneur is the word to describe me, but it's not a good word. Used-car dealer? That sounds evil but has a nice ring to it. I don't remember what I put on my passport. Company director probably. It covers a multitude of sins. But I work hard for whatever I've got, seven days a week, from when I get up to when I go to bed.

Bernie Ecclestone

We're in show business.

Bernie Ecclestone

Dad taught me everything I know, but he would never tell me anything he knew.

Al Unser Jr, on his father

If marriage is the only war in which you sleep with the enemy, so Grand Prix racing is the only sport in which your main rival is your team-mate. He alone has the same equipment; he alone is the true yardstick.

Nigel Roebuck, motor racing writer

I've never thought the grass was greener on the other side – just a different shade of brown really. I suppose that's why I've always been one of the more cheerful drivers. You need to be like that because the hardest races are the ones where you get out of the car after driving to a finish, and you're physically and mentally destroyed. You've lost maybe seven or eight pounds of weight with the heat. Your hands are blistered and your legs have gone dead. But all you've done is finish seventh. No points. You walk to the pits unnoticed. That's very difficult.

Derek Warwick

Movement is tranquillity.

Stirling Moss

When one runs the risk of losing a sense of proportion, it's time to go home, sleep in the same bed in which one dreamed while still a nobody, and to eat the simple, healthy dishes of one's childhood.

Juan Fangio, *Fangio*

You must always believe you will become the best, but you must never believe you have done so.

Juan Fangio

You know you have arrived in life when you get your name printed on the side of your cap.

David Coulthard

Motor racing belongs in England.

Ron Dennis

The most awesome old fart I know.

A friend, on A. J. Foyt

I'm proud of what I have achieved but I'm not trying to prove women can do everything. I'm just trying to prove Lyn St James can do it.

Lyn St James, IndyCar driver

Nigel Mansell is quick – but he's a bit like James Hunt – a frustrated Spitfire pilot.

Motor-racing fan

This is something I have been thinking about for four years. My feeling is that the Isle of Man has given me so much I want to put something back into the community.

Nigel Mansell, announcing his recruitment as a Special Constable on the Isle of Man

Drag racing can be dangerous. If you make a mistake in the work with trees and pylons you'll get a free X-ray and a crinkly hairdo.

Robin Read, drag racer

Tyre shake is the worst thing. If the tyres start wobbling badly, at best you can't see a thing. At worst the [cerebral] cortex can be shaken loose.

Robin Read, drag racer

The truth, then, is this; no one of importance in the sport ever really wanted Nigel Mansell to make it. He spoke the wrong brand of English, he broke the rules of success. He represented hard work and thrusting honesty in a world made for sycophants.

Profile of Nigel Mansell in *The Observer*

Emerson Fittipaldi was my hero and my example, but he was only a dream when I was about 13 or 14. I never thought that I could one day be like that, or be even more successful. So it has been a dream which has become a reality . . . but with some nightmares in the middle. Such is life. Nothing is smooth.

Ayrton Senna

Someone said that you need two lives; one to make mistakes in, the other to enjoy. Well, I feel I could do with three or four.

Ayrton Senna

It was a soul-destroying decision to take. It has taken us four years to fight our way to the front. I am very angry.

Ted Toleman, announcing his withdrawal from Formula One

You know, after Monza and Estoril last year, I went home to think about things. And I said to myself, it is like you have a cheque book and you write them out, one after another to the angels. And then one day you have an empty book and you cannot give them out again.

Gerhard Berger

He left the team under a cloud. But clouds blow away and I'm sure that's what will happen.

Frank Williams, after Nigel Mansell left the team

One side of me says go away from this and look after yourself, the other side says you love it, it's been your life, you get so much out of it and you've got the respect of so many people all over the world, you just can't drop it.

Ayrton Senna, in 1993

> Good eyes, bald head, quick hands.
> I have a beautiful friend
> And I thought the old despair
> Would end in love in the end.
> But I looked into your eyes one day
> And saw her image there
> And have gone weeping away.

A poem by fan Shelagh Poulter-Marron for Stirling Moss

Just stand along the pit wall, listen to the noise, smell rubber smoking and oil burning. You'll be hooked for life.

Derek Warwick

No one loses anything or does anything for someone else. We live in a vast prison like Kafka's. The world is a penitentiary and we are the inmates; caught in an instinctive egotism, we have to depend on our own force and nothing else. Whatever we pretend, we value others not for the good they can do us, but for the evil they might. The man who might kill us receives our full attention. He requires it, for we live in a cruel world where violence has taken the place of reason, a world where the only positive element is fear, the chief instrument of power.

Enzo Ferrari

SPARES

Serious sport has nothing to do with fair play. It is bound up with hatred, jealousy, boastfulness, disregard of all rules and sadistic pleasure in witnessing violence; in other words it is war minus the shooting.

George Orwell, 'The Sporting Spirit'

Image-making is a risk. I've questioned myself about it and I've tried to be an ostrich and ignore other people's glamorous, distorted view of me as much as I can. Limelight's a danger and so is wealth. It's like giving a dog a big juicy bone. When he didn't have one he could live without it, but, once he's tasted one, he hangs on like grim death.

James Hunt

I've tried to hide the fact that I had a title but ever since then I can honestly say I've never come up against this Earl thing within the sport. Everyone accepts me for what I am, a racing driver, and that is gratifying.

Johnny Dumfries, then the Earl of Dumfries, now the Marquess of Bute

Before the race began, I was so nervous I asked the team if they could go out in the crowd and find a short guy with a moustache to put in the car.

Nigel Mansell, after the 1994 Phoenix IndyCar race

Before my father died I wanted to have much more of him than I actually got. Whatever it is you are missing in the early days, you end up striving for the rest of your life.

Damon Hill

The arrogance of a god makes him drive like a demon.

Hugh McIlvanney, on Ayrton Senna

It's a terrible time for motor racing, but you cannot choose when you receive the great chance of your life. I'm in a tunnel this weekend, there's no doubt about it.

David Coulthard, on taking the drive after Ayrton Senna's accident

Motor sport can be regarded as the test bed of the motor industry, helping to develop the technology of tomorrow's passenger car.

Kenneth Clark, MP, then Minister for Trade and Industry

I have an idea for a ballet, the central theme a thesis; I don't know where I'm going, but I will be there ahead of you. Driving is a dance, in a way, the same, but never the same, never monotonous. Monotony in life would drive me mad. I can't bear inactivity . . . I fill every moment. When you leave me here Ken Gregory and some people are coming for a meeting. After that I'm going out to dinner. Then I'm going dancing. I don't know how long I'll stay out, but one thing I'm sure of, when I go to bed tonight I hope to be very tired, because I don't want to think. I don't like thinking unless it's about a specific solvable problem. As far as life is concerned, and what life is going to offer me, I find it terribly depressing . . . I know that to some people achievement in business, in work, is happiness . . . My idea of happiness seems Utopian to me and it may seem absurd to you, but it is to be married, and have two or three children, and a house in the country, if you like, and to go away for two weeks on holiday – and most of all, most importantly, to be able to accept that life as happiness. Do you understand? To be able to *accept* it, that's the whole heart of the matter.

Stirling Moss

The one thing I have is this dream, that I will return to racing all dressed in black and nobody knows who I am and I win everything.

Trevor Taylor

I don't want them to become too fond of me. One of these days, I may not come back again and they will suffer less if I keep them a bit at arm's length.

Alberto Ascari on his children (Richard Garrett, *The Motor Racing Story*)

I miss not being there a great deal. I miss the testing, the worrying, the talking long into the night. Could this go wrong, could that? Have we got it right here? What are the others doing?

Frank Williams

People who cheat only cheat themselves.

Bernie Ecclestone

Infatuation is one of the evils of the world, whether it's for a woman or a sport. I race because it's the one thing I can do better than anything else. I could give it up if I wanted to.

Jackie Stewart

Mark, my younger son, was not particularly keen on the idea and Paul, 13, was amazed that anybody should be interested at all.

Jackie Stewart, rejecting an offer to return to motor racing

My hope is we don't ever get too big and lose some of that mystique. I'm mindful that we don't grow into something austere.

Eddie Jordan

I only look forward. What point is there in keeping trophies?

Niki Lauda, who gives all his trophies to his local garage in return for free car washes

Before I retire or leave Ferrari I want to go to a restaurant, anywhere in Italy, and be allowed to pay for a meal.

Nigel Mansell

It's a week now since I had the call from Frank Williams and I still don't understand why he told me he wasn't interested. I'm hoping he actually meant 'not yet' when he called me and said, point blank, 'no way'.

Martin Brundle

He deserves to win a world title. But why must he always play himself up and play the car down? This is not correct towards Patrick Head and the other 100 people who help Mansell win his races.

Keke Rosberg, on Nigel Mansell

Faldo's got more nerve than me. I couldn't do what he does. Golfers are visible to everyone. Their sport is harder than mine.

Nigel Mansell, an accomplished golfer, on Nick Faldo

SPARES

Being in an English prison for two months has cost me almost £1 million. This must be the most expensive accommodation in Europe. It is certainly the least attractive.

Belgian driver Bertrand Gachot, freed from prison on appeal after being jailed for 18 months for spraying a taxi driver with CS gas

If you scrape off all the gloss, our biggest asset is our ability to finish.

Ron Dennis

Your justice scandalises Europe. Better a spray in London than a dagger in Heysel.

Banner unveiled outside the British embassy in Brussels after the jailing of Bertrand Gachot

Even when the pressure and the problems really get inside me, I never lose a feeling that I belong to an extremely privileged group of men.

John Watson

Once I have my first race under my belt it will be a relief. I know I have had a lucky break and that there are other brilliant young drivers out there who would love my seat, but I have done my homework. I know what it's like to finish putting my bike together late at night, hitch up the trailer before going on a long drive to the meeting, pitch a tent in the freezing cold and then fall off the thing attempting to qualify the following morning.

Damon Hill

I always thought he would be a solicitor or an accountant.

Bette Hill, mother of Damon

How about the speed merchants? How do professional motor drivers escape?

> Mr William Keenan, MP, inquiring about the possible evasion of National Service by motor racing drivers in the fifties.

When I hear of these young, daring, courageous people going abroad racing round tracks to the danger of their lives, and when I hear of their physical incapacity I wonder. What bewilders me is whether they are likely to encounter, because of their inferior physical capacity, greater hardship, inconvenience, and discomfort while undertaking National Service than when racing round dirt and motor tracks of other countries.

> Emmanuel Shinwell, later Lord Shinwell, on the same issue during a debate in the House of Commons on 'call-up dodgers'

You can tell by instinct when something is going on. You know by the frequency of telephone calls, by the body language and the eye contact. In many ways it's no different from going out to a nightclub and casting your eye across the dance floor.

> Eddie Jordan, on telltale signs when other teams are trying to entice his drivers away

We are a nation of dreamers and fantasists, but in some of our visions reality doesn't play a major part. It's the difference between last thing at night and first thing in the morning. You will never know what you are capable of until you try, but you have got to keep in touch with reality. It's very easy to lie to yourself and you must be totally honest.

> Eddie Jordan, Irishman

Before I retire or leave Ferrari I want to go to a restaurant, anywhere in Italy, and be allowed to pay for a meal.

Nigel Mansell

We're too sophisticated for American audiences. Their television coverage is like all-in wrestling. I would hate to see our sport Americanised.

Bernie Ecclestone

I carry out my business in a very unusual way. I don't like contracts. I like to be able to look someone in the eye and then shake them by the hand rather than do it the American way with 92-page contracts that no one reads or understands. If I say I'll do something, then I'll do it; if I say I won't, then I won't. Surprisingly, people seem to like that.

Bernie Ecclestone

At the moment, Ayrton is like an angel to me. He is up there alongside God, looking down on me. I know that is a child's way of thinking, but it works for me.

Rubens Barrichello

Like all sportsmen I have become a prisoner of my sport. It's not that I'm anti-social or a hermit. But if I leave this hotel room I know I will not be able to do what I want. There's no freedom. It's difficult to have a normal conversation. The world we live in is so unreal. That is why it is important to come home, plant your feet on the ground, and realise what the real world is all about.

Nigel Mansell

Maybe I will do something good with my life one day. We are such bloody funny people, we human beings.

Nelson Piquet

He's got his finger on the pulse of everything. If there's a Formula Libre driver in Zaire looking for a drive, you can be sure Eddie will know about him.

Stefan Johansson, on Eddie Jordan

I reckon I am doing more for Britain this way than I would by being called up.

Peter Collins, on the possibility of being called up for National Service

I get twitched if I have to go three or four days without a girl. But I get twitched if I'm three or four days out of my car.

Rupert Keegan

That may be good enough for the American public, with their hotdogs and hamburgers, but it is not good enough for fans of European car racing.

Jean-Marie Balestre, criticising proposed reforms in Formula One

My father was very bright to stop my mother calling me Hamish. Stirling Moss is the name that sticks. It helped.

Stirling Moss

When I first came into Formula One I thought Ron Dennis was a God. Then, after we were ahead of McLaren for most of last season, I realised he was just another human being.

Flavio Briatore, boss of Benetton

I make a lot of jokes about the fact that as a neurosurgeon I should hardly be required at a motor race because the drivers don't have any brains, otherwise they wouldn't race.

Prof. Sidney Watkins, head of the medical panel for the International Motor Sports Federation

To see your kids go from toddlers to the starting grid with you, then run one-two and share so many precious moments, from a personal side they have no equal in satisfaction. Sometimes I have to pinch myself when I realise that we did it over and over, not just one lucky shot. What a prize. When I look back on the memories, none of the negatives of the sport make any impact.

Mario Andretti

You will travel faster still through the Heavens.

Inscription on the vault of the grave of Tazio Nuvolari in Mantua

I'm not particularly worried about meeting Michael Jackson, but I do enjoy it when Stirling Moss is around.

Nick Mason, drummer with Pink Floyd and a part-time racer

When I first started racing, it was a real redneck situation. You did not dare bring your wife or girlfriend because half the people were drunk and the rest were fighting.

Stock-car racer Richard Petty

There are no supermen. Everyone puts his pants on one leg at a time.

Rick Mears

What we are doing must be confusing the other teams. I know it must because it's confusing me.

Eddie Jordan, on his then shoestring operation

Mind you it's good for business. People feel so sorry for me they let me get away with murder.

Frank Williams, on his paralysis

My dad once said you meet a much nicer class of person there but I'm not so sure. I had a few hairy moments getting by people.

Damon Hill, after having to start at the back of the grid in the 1993 Portuguese Grand Prix

If you have God on your side everything becomes clear. I have a blessing from Him. But of course, I can get hurt or killed as anyone can.

Ayrton Senna

The paddock and the pit lane have about as much to do with the jet set these days as cauliflower cheese. Sure, you may have George Harrison or Chris Evans wandering around, but, mostly, it's full to overflowing with photocopier salesmen in metal suits on corporate hospitality dos. The wives, called Debi-Ann, are to be found tottering about on stupendously high heels and being rude to security people, partly because they're nasty, and partly because they think they're one of the grander film stars. In fact, the only reason they're there is because their husband, Colin, sold more photocopiers than anyone last month.

Jeremy Clarkson, journalist

People usually expect to meet some gigantic side of beef, you know? A superstrong, tobacco-chewing, grease-under-the-fingernails person. Sometimes if people don't know what I do, I don't tell them because I know they'll argue with me – 'You are not!'

Lyn St James, IndyCar driver

To do something well is so worth while that to die trying to do it better cannot be foolhardy. Life is measured in achievement not in years alone.

Bruce McLaren

The only place where my father has been an issue is in England. There was an effect, when, for example, I was at the Bar or trying to do anything of that kind. As soon as I went into motorsport, even in England, it was zero. The first time I noticed this was at a club race, about the third time I ever did one. They were reading out the names and somebody said, 'Mosley? He must be some relation to Alf Mosley, the coach builder from Leicester.' As soon as I heard that I realised I'd found the right place.

Max Mosley, the son of the pre-war Fascist leader Sir Oswald Mosley

When I smoke – I'm choosy. Craven 'A' give me all I want of a smoke – and nothing I don't.

Part of the copy for an advertisment by Stirling Moss

Eddie Jordan could offload a consignment of Albanian word processors on Del Boy Trotter, trade a prospective MOT test failure to Arthur Daley. He was born to sell sand to sheikhs, send coals to Newcastle.

Michael Calvin, journalist

An enterprise which, although condemned at its inception by self-proclaimed cognoscenti as amateurish, became everything I might have wished of a Formula One equipe. Efficient but never hardfaced, competitive but never devious, stylish but never arrogant. James, more than anyone, reflected this Corinthian ethos.

Lord Hesketh's description of his team, at the memorial service for James Hunt

Letting my wife go shopping by herself.

Michael Andretti's reply when asked what was the craziest thing he
had ever done at Monte Carlo

I am convinced they will not want to race. They have been
brought up with love and security. They will not need to
prove their superiority to their friends; they will not be
complex characters in that way.

Niki Lauda, on his children

Jackie screeched into the pits and started moaning about
something in the engine not quite sparking or something. I
stuck my head into his cockpit. 'Calm down,' I said. 'You
think you've got problems. Well, let me tell you that England
lost four wickets before lunch to the Aussies at the Oval and
now they've just lost Ken Barrington.'

Ken Tyrrell, on Jackie Stewart

Cocaine is God's way of telling you you're making too much
money. And a lot of people in glamour industries have
used it. In fact, I'm forever comparing motor racing and
the music business. In many way James Hunt was like an
elder statesman of pop. Look at people like Clapton and
Townshend: they've been through the same drug and drink
thing. The two industries are so alike. The only big difference
is that there's more money in motor racing and a far higher
class of groupie.

John Giddings, a friend of James Hunt

If God wanted us to walk, he'd have given us pogo sticks
instead of feet. Feet are made to fit car pedals.

Stirling Moss

Who do you think you are, Nigel Mansell?
No, actually I'm Ayrton Senna.

> Conversation between a policeman and Ayrton Senna over speeding

Ayrton waves me down and I thought of running him over, perhaps breaking his big toe. But like a good RAC man I stopped.

> Nigel Mansell, after giving his arch rival Ayrton Senna a lift on his car at the end of the 1991 British Grand Prix

Well, it's not bad, is it? Senna having one of our cars in his mirrors.

> Eddie Jordan, on Andrea de Cesaris's fourth place in the 1991 Mexican Grand Prix

This has been a fantastic experience for me. I've loved every second of it. Perhaps now people will stop taking me for a stupid actor who is simply playing at racing and accept me as a serious racer. That's what I want more than anything else.

> Actor Paul Newman, after coming second in the 1979 Le Mans race

The only times I've minded the 'only woman' thing have been when I've finished 12th or whatever in a race, but still been invited on to the podium because I was the highest-placed woman driver. I didn't deserve to be there.

> Lyn St James, IndyCar driver

Now a car comes in, you can't see it for mechanics . . . We want girls around the paddock, not all these boring men and that includes me.

> Flavio Briatore

This Williams team is what, a £25 million business? Does anyone believe they would have given me one of their two cars last year because years ago someone there had known my dad?

Damon Hill

Adrenalin is a great pain-killer.

Nigel Mansell

Bravery isn't hard to find. Skill is something else again. Drivers who have only courage don't last for long.

Stirling Moss

It was at the bottom of our hearts to dedicate this victory to our great friend Ayrton Senna. He brought so much happiness to Brazil and this was our only opportunity to do the same.

Claudio Taffarel, the Brazilian goalkeeper, after his country won the 1994 World Cup

I have my young baby son in my heart but we have also Ayrton as part of us. This would have been his fourth title this year and now we have won the World Cup four times. His hand and the hand of God were upon us.

Brazilian football star Bebeto

In one word, very exciting.

Nigel Mansell, expressing his feeling on his return to Formula One

I love having beautiful women around. It is an essential part of motor racing

Alain de Cadenet, former racing driver

**Who do you think you are, Nigel Mansell?
No, actually I'm Ayrton Senna.**

Conversation between a policeman and Ayrton Senna over
speeding

The fact that I'm the Prime Minister's son doesn't always help. At Le Mans, for instance, at almost 200 mph down the Mulsanne Straight, maybe in the rain, Mum can't fix it if the brakes fail.

Mark Thatcher

Nigel? . . . Mmm. Well there's no question that we'll miss him. There's no doubt the guy is immensely quick. But unlike Alan Jones and Keke Rosberg, who won races with us, I have no fond memories. There are moments when you sit in the office and daydream and remember the good times. Sure, every relationship has a lot of ups and downs but, in Nigel's case, there seemed to be a lot of downs. But, in the car, he was a brilliant driver. He made last year's car go very quickly – I mean he was often faster than the car. That frequently masked problems with it.

Frank Williams, on Nigel Mansell's departure in 1989

After you've had Alain Prost and Ayrton Senna as team-mates you don't give a f*** who the next bloke is.

Damon Hill

Without racing I would be dead within three years.

Teddy Yip (Gerald Donaldson, *Gilles Villeneuve*)

I know that no human being can perform miracles, but Gilles made you wonder sometimes.

Jacques Laffite, on Gilles Villeneuve (ibid.)

Next to my dad and uncle Bobby the drivers I most admired while growing up were A. J. Foyt and Gordon Johncock and when I passed them and my dad it was like I lost something and at the same time became one of them.

Al Unser Jr (Kris Perkins, *IndyCar*)

I once worked for Lola as a cook. The sponsors wanted frightfully pretentious food, the drivers only ate pasta in case they got squits in their race suits, and the mechanics always had baked beans.

Claire Latimer, former caterer to John Major

Being passed by you and following your car is a true lesson in itself, and every time I follow you round the course, I learn something new.

Giuseppe Farina, to Tazio Nuvolari (Prince Bira, *Bits and Pieces*)

Racing in Japan was small and so I bought myself a ticket to Paris, because I thought it was the capital of England.

Ukyo Katayama

Perhaps when USA '94 is over, he might like to turn his attention to rallying. He could sort out the kit-car rules, find a way to reduce the huge costs of top-class rallying and, with his now legendary business acumen, fund a scholarship scheme in Ireland to help find the next generation of Fishers, McKinstrys and McHales.

Keith Oswin, journalist, on Jackie Charlton

My boy, you have seen my car and my organisation – with my team and my factory, we will make you World Champion. Fucka the championship, how mucha you pay?

Conversation between Louis Stanley and Clay Regazzoni (Alan Jones, *Alan Jones – Driving Ambition*)

The silk scarves and the blondes on the arm are the raw meat you feed to an animal; namely, the public.

Alan Jones (ibid.)

SPARES

I hate the big time. I feel the loss of close friends terribly. I have to have bouncers at my birthday parties now.

James Hunt (Frank Keating, *Caught by Keating*)

Life is a journey whose meaning is as much *in* the journey as *in* the end.

Peter Revson, *Speed With Style*

What has changed most in the years I have been observing the sport is style, the style of the people involved. I have watched drivers, constructors, sponsors, officials, PR men, advertisers, groupies and almost everyone grow rich; I have watched their progressive alienation from both their roots and the sport. I have watched their lives grow more sumptuous and their souls more stressful.

Keith Botsford, *The Champions of Formula One*

If a man can f*** and drive race cars, man . . . I mean, what else is there?

Bill Scott, stock-car racer (Jonathon Green and Don Atyeo, *The Book of Sports Quotes*)

Since 1950, my Ferrari has shown an Italy which is not solely represented by spaghetti and music.

Enzo Ferrari (ibid.)

I drive the car, I don't carry it.

Janet Guthrie, the first woman to qualify for the Indianapolis 500, responding when asked if she was strong enough to compete in motor racing (ibid.)

The engine that's behind us in our racing cars,
It don't run run, Ron, it don't run, Ron!
It's got us through the qualifying laps so far,
But it don't run run, Ron, it don't run, Ron!
Ahhh! It gets us in the race,
Ahhh! Then it's egg on face,
Ahhh! It can't take the pace!
It don't run run, Ron, it don't run, Ron!
Love and kisses
Marty and Mika.

Letter to *Autosport* by Adam Warne

I miss the camaraderie between the drivers. We all hung out together, and went to the nightclubs and bars after the race. In F1 everyone just disappears. It's like you're raping a country. You go in, do the race, and get out before you get caught. That's what it feels like.

Eddie Irvine, contrasting racing in Japan with Formula One

Senna: we accelerate together. The fourth title is ours.

Inscription on a banner held by Brazilian football supporters

Ben Hur – his chariot had less horsepower than the Williams, but he still won.

Johnny Herbert, on the person in history he mostly strongly identifies with

He was always crazy, like with snowmobiles, helicopters, four-by-four jeeps or whatever. He would go out there and kill the thing, then repair it in his garage, then go out and kill it again. In his skiing he was always trying to jump this and jump that. He wasn't a very good skier, but he still skied like a madman.

Jacques Villeneuve, on his father Gilles

SPARES

A woman should always stress her true femininity, whatever her occupation. Even on rallies, choked with dust and with our faces smeared with soot and grease, whenever we can spare a minute we pull in for a quick wash and tidy up.

Nancy Mitchell, rally driver in the 1950s

It often seems to me that art and motor racing balance my life perfectly. After the excitement of speed on the track I go to the quietness, the calm of the studio. It is a balanced, symmetrical life.

Price Bira, who was also a noted sculptor

People say I'm tough and that my drivers fear me, and maybe they do. But all I'm doing is letting them know that when they are managed by me there are certain standards I expect of them. If they can't or won't put up with that then they pay the price.

Eddie Jordan

Mon ami mate.

How Mike Hawthorn and Peter Collins referred to each other during their time in Italy

I left for England where the BRM officials welcomed me with an enthusiasm unusual in that land of understatement.

Juan Fangio, *Fangio*

There are two options in this game of ours, neither of them very appealing. You can quit racing and save your life, or you can quit racing and lose what life is about.

François Cevert (Frank Keating, *Long Days, Late Nights*)

159

On top of that came the CBE, which was most unexpected. I remember picking up this envelope marked '10 Downing Street' and thinking, 'Oh damn, Mark Thatcher's after a drive.'

Robin Herd (Mike Lawrence, *The Story of March*)

He belongs to the pool room and the bar room, and looks like a brimming toby jug, though it is obvious no mantelpiece would hold him.

Louis Stanley, on Tom Wheatcroft (Louis Stanley, *Grand Prix: The Legendary Years*)

If we were in Germany and he was on pole position, and I overtook him and led him halfway around the lap, how do you think he'd feel about it? You know, if I led into the stadium on the parade lap, he'd be a bit miffed wouldn't he? It was quite extraordinary, so he brought it on himself, that one.

Damon Hill, on Michael Schumacher, who overtook Hill on the parade lap at the 1994 British Grand Prix

Any girl, attractive as well as being a capable driver, who had a few glamour tricks up your sleeve and 'crowd appeal' could race today and pull in a four-figure income.

Kay Petre, motor racing and rally driver in the 1930s

Style is *very* important. It's the manner in which you conduct yourself, a means of achieving things, the way you handle yourself.

Peter Revson, *Speed With Style*

Fangio.

The title of a tango composed by Javier Mazzea

SPARES

If he had studied, if he had gone to university, I bet you anything he would have been a Nobel Prize winner.

> Enrico Vannini, journalist, on Juan Fangio (Juan Fangio with Roberto Carozzo, *My Racing Life*)

You could sum it up by saying that motor racing used to be gentlemen trying to be mechanics, whereas nowadays motor racing is mechanics pretending to be gentlemen.

> Innes Ireland (Peter Manso, *Vroom*)

I suppose you'll be as proud of me as I am of you.

> Yuri Gargarin, the first man in space, to Jim Clark (Graham Gauld, *Jim Clark – The Legend Lives On*)

Johnny Needs A Fast Car.

> Title of song written by Chris Rea about Johnny Herbert

I want to be where Williams and Benetton are: at the more intellectual stage, at the mental boundary.

> Nick Wirth, boss of Simtek

But I leave IndyCar racing very satisfied. I came across, I endured, I competed, I won.

> Nigel Mansell

A most polite and luxurious kidnapping . . . My captors kept apologising to me and they served me breakfast in bed.

> Juan Fangio, describing his kidnapping by Fidel Castro's July 26 Movement in 1958

So they think I'm an old fart, do they? Well tell them I'm back and that I mean business.

> Nigel Mansell

I loved being with him, even if it meant following him around for hours. He liked shooting and would usually let me tag along and load for him. It wasn't much but it gave me the chance to see the effect he had on people. Once the Queen turned up on a shoot and everyone stiffened except for my father. He didn't exactly say 'Wotcha Queenie!' but being a natural show-off he dealt with it in a slightly irreverent way. Nothing fazed him.

    Damon Hill on his father

Given the opportunity, I can go and win another world championship without batting an eye. I can beat Schumacher. I can beat anyone. Believe me, when you have won a world championship and you have won all those races, you know how to get the job done.

    Nigel Mansell

Like an addict who just cannot get enough, Formula One injected a final shot of controversy into a season that everyone thought had ended when officials at the international motor sport federation (FIA) leaked the news yesterday that they were considering summoning Michael Schumacher and Damon Hill to a disciplinary hearing in Paris to discuss their collison during the Australian Grand Prix.

    Oliver Holt, journalist

Throughout my career, whenever there was trouble, it made me stronger.

    Michael Schumacher

Damon [Hill] talks about being confident, but Michael [Schumacher] just is.

    Martin Brundle

Lies, intrigue and lawyers; fines, bans and fires; confusion, hypocrisy and cheating. It hasn't been a good season for Grand Prix motor racing, has it? Nothing has gone right from the moment the Grand Prix circus assembled in Brazil back in March, and I'm beginning to wonder if any real racing has taken place.

Denis Jenkinson, journalist, on the 1994 season

It is a cataclysimic withdrawal I'm feeling right now. It's like losing yourself and it's not going to be easy without them. My heart will leave the sport because I've lost them both.

Paul Newman, actor and partner of the Newman Haas IndyCar team, on the return to Formula One of Nigel Mansell and the retirement of Mario Andretti

Everybody thought of us as a T-shirt company. Racing is a very closed club. We stirred things up when we started winning. There's a lot of resentment.

Flavio Briatore, boss of Benetton

If I were a betting man and had $100,000, I would put it on Michael Schumacher. That's not to undermine Damon but, looking at it dispassionately and statistically, he has to upset the odds.

Patrick Head, technical director of Williams, in the week coming up to the last race of the 1994 season in Australia

People come back from Monaco and say 'I drove the circuit'. I believe it will not be long before they say the same thing of Birmingham.

Martin Hone, who hoped to stage Formula One Races in Birmingham

A most polite and luxurious kidnapping . . . My captors kept apologising to me and they served me breakfast in bed.

Juan Fangio, describing his kidnapping by Fidel Castro's July 26 Movement in 1958